ADVENTURES WITH THE ANABAPTISTS

by Jeanne Grieser and Carol Duerksen

Faith & Life
Resources

A Division of Mennonite
Publishing House

Adventures with the Anabaptists introduces youth to the events and personalities of the radical reformers of the early 16th century in Europe. The 10-session study, written for teachers and including reproducible sheets, brings history to life, relating it to the contemporary issues youth face.

Printed in the United States of America
01 02 03 04 05 06 6 5 4 3 2 1
International Standard Book Number 0-8361-9211-7

Editorial direction for Faith & Life Resources by Byron Rempel-Burkholder; editorial consultant, Abe Bergen; copyediting by Edna Krueger Dyck; cover and design by Jim. L. Friesen; printing by Mennonite Press, Newton, Kansas.

Cover art: Engravings from the *Martyrs Mirror* (Scottdale, Pa: Herald Press, 1938) and Mirror of the Martyrs' exhibit, Bethel College, Newton, Kan. Used by permission. Portraits of Conrad Grebel, Felix Manz, and George Blaurock painted by Oliver Wendell Schenk; reproductions reprinted by permission of Laurelville Mennonite Church Center, Mt. Pleasant, Pa. Painting of Menno Simons, also by Oliver Wendell Schenk; reproduction reprinted by permission of Eastern Mennonite University.

Unless otherwise noted, Scripture text is from the New Revised Standard Version, copyright © 1989, Division of Christian Education of the National Council of Churches in Christ in the United States of America.

TABLE OF CONTENTS

INTRODUCTION

Anabaptists. The rebaptizers. The men and women with enough courage to be burned alive for their faith. The forefathers and mothers of the "peace churches" today. The folks who believed that faith and discipleship can't be separated. The outspoken people who witnessed openly and freely about the love of Jesus.

Perhaps you've heard bits and pieces of the stories of Felix Manz, Conrad Grebel, Menno Simons, and a host of other Anabaptists. Maybe you've seen the thick volume, *Martyrs Mirror,* and even read a story or two. But in reality, how much do you know? And how much do the young people in your congregation know? For that matter, does it matter?

Yes. It matters because where we come from affects who we are <u>and where we are going</u>. Our past informs our present and leads us into the future. In today's volatile world, where individuals and countries must respond to unprovoked violence, it behooves us to see how our Anabaptist brothers and sisters responded to the violence perpetrated against them. It behooves us to study their Schleitheim Confession. Is this still what we believe? And if so, what are we doing about it today?

We welcome you to this adventure in learning about the Anabaptists, and we believe that even though this curriculum is written to be taught to junior and senior high youth, you will be excited about how much you learn yourself.

Other Resources

In addition to the material you'll find in this booklet, we suggest several additional resources that can help enhance your study series. There is an extensive bibliography on page 95. Of those resources, we encourage you to consider using several in particular, which should be obtained as soon as possible from your church library, resource center, bookstore, or direct order from Faith & Life Resources at 1-800-245-7894.

1) The best source for deeper historical background is *Through Fire and Water* (Herald Press, 1995). This is an overview of Mennonite history, co-authored by Harry Loewen and Steven Nolt. The book is invaluable, providing insights and information on the early

Anabaptists. Many of the Digging Deeper sections rely heavily upon it. We strongly suggest you make the book part of your preparation for teaching.

2) We also suggest that you use the video "The Radicals" as part of teaching this curriculum (see Session 6). This hour-long drama by Gateway Films/Vision Video portrays the young Anabaptist movement, and particularly the life of the martyrs Michael and Margaretha Sattler. This film has some violent scenes in it and you may want to preview it and let parents know if you plan to show it to their young people.

3) To decorate your meeting place, you may wish to display posters of Tom Schenk's attractive paintings of Menno Simons, Conrad Grebel, George Blaurock, and Felix Manz (shown on the cover).

4) For some sessions, we refer to other resources, such as the *Martyrs Mirror* and a shorter retelling of some of the *Mirror's* stories, *On Fire for Christ*, by Dave and Neta Jackson. Especially in Session 5, you will want to be prepared to share these martyr stories.

Make It Fun

Finally, we encourage you to have fun with this curriculum. Whether you are playing "To Tell the Truth" with the youth in Session 2 or performing the skit "Menno Who?" in Session 7, enjoy it and help the youth have a good time too. You can have the same rewarding experience Carol did when her class was playing "To Tell the Truth." Class time was up and she told them they could go or finish the last round of the game. They wanted to stay.

(Editor's note: Although Carol's name appears on the cover because she worked with the manuscript, she says she remembers more from ten weeks of test-teaching *Adventures with the Anabaptists* than from editing the book. Why? Because one was reading only, while the other included leading the lessons and doing activities.)

If you enjoy teaching this adventure, and your class wants to stay to learn more, then God has done great things. Blessings to you!

—Jeanne Grieser and Carol Duerksen

"A Change in the Church" introduces youth to Martin Luther, some of his reasons for disagreeing with the Catholic Church of the 16th Century, and what he did to launch the Protestant Reformation, of which the Anabaptists were a radical wing.	**SESSION 1**
"Three Men and a Bible" introduces youth to Conrad Grebel, Felix Manz, and Geroge Blaurock, and how their lives where dramatically changed through reading the Bible.	**SESSION 2**
"The Great Debate" invites youth to become involved with the choices that were at the heart of the early debates between the radical reformers and the state church.	**SESSION 3**
"The ReBaptizers" offers background to the Anabaptists' insistence on believer's baptism, and helps youth think about baptism today.	**SESSION 4**
In "Blessed Are the Picked On" youth will learn that persecution and martyrdom were part of the price the Anabaptists paid for their faith.	**SESSION 5**
"This We Believe" helps the youth become familiar with the Schleitheim Confession, and encourages them to examine their own beliefs in light of that statement. The story of Michael Sattler is woven into this session.	**SESSION 6**
"Promises, Promises" explores the promise of God's presence with us when we celebrate the Lord's Supper. The unit introduces Menno Simons through a look at the struggles he had with the official church's teaching on Communion.	**SESSION 7**
"Peace It Together" introduces youth to the pacifist position that was a significant part of what most of the Anabaptists believed, and invites them to consider what it means to be peacemakers today.	**SESSION 8**
"A Servant Leader" portrays Jesus' style of leadership, using Menno Simons as an example. Youth will be challenged to live out the Anabaptist values of sacrificial love and service.	**SESSION 9**
"One Foundation" introduces Menno Simons' theme verse and the fact that Jesus Christ is indeed our one foundation for faith and life.	**SESSION 10**

HOW TO | TEACH THIS COURSE

The lesson structure used in this study is borrowed from the Fast Lane Bible studies, a youth curriculum also published by Faith & Life Resources. As outlined in more detail below under "Lesson Structure," the teaching begins with a life focus. After discussing a common situation teens may experience, we search the faith story for clues about what God has to say about the issue. Then we return to the life situation and consider practical applications and responses.

Consistent with the Anabaptists' identity as "people of the book," we want the youth to understand the biblical basis for the Anabaptists' actions and beliefs. Scripture is used in every session, as part of the faith story. Still, you will find that the lessons quickly move to the stories of the Anabaptists. Often they are offered in the form of a skit or dramatic reading. For these to be effective, we urge that you, the teacher, immerse yourself in the passion and the excitement of the stories. Become familiar with the suggested background reading (noted in the introduction). Enlist others in the congregation and the youth group to help you tell the stories well.

The Anabaptist story includes great drama, much suffering, and intense feelings about issues of faith. These will come through in this session. At the same time, the writers often use appropriate humor to draw students into reflection and discussion. They suggest a variety of activities, from discussion, to skits, to artwork, thus addressing the variety of learning styles that is found within most groups. Feel free to adopt their ideas to your group's character and circumstances, but we encourage you to keep the learning time fun and group oriented.

A final idea: You may wish to offer the students materials to maintain a scrapbook or folder of handouts and exercises used in the curriculum. This keepsake could also include extra paper for journaling during the week. The scrapbook is an option you will need to develop in a way that fits your group and the personalities within it. You will need to give some thought as to how you want to incorporate it into the lessons, since the outlines do not include further guidelines.

USING THE | TEACHER'S GUIDE

LESSON STRUCTURE

The following is a summary of how the lessons are organized:

PREPARATION

Orient yourself to the lesson by reading through the Preparation section. Here you will find the central focus of the lesson as well as a teaching goal..

Scripture text

The session is connected to this Bible passage. Read through it to gain a sense of what the text is saying. What strikes you as you read it?

Faith focus

This is the story of the Scripture passage in a nutshell. Here is the nugget of truth on which we will focus this lesson.

Session goal

As you teach, be aware of your goal. What outcomes of this lesson—changes in knowledge, attitude, or action—do you desire in your students?

Materials and advance preparation needed

You will find a list of what you will need to carry through the suggested lesson plan. Glance over this part a week before you teach this lesson.

EXPLORATION

Carefully follow the five step-by-step movements through the lesson. They will carry you from life to the faith story, and back to life. The variety of activities should appeal to different kinds of learners and keep your students from getting bored.

1. Focus. This movement serves two purposes: to create a friendly climate in the classroom and to focus attention on the session's topic. Usually this beginning step will be interactive and fun.

2. Connect. Here the student's experience is connected to the issue. In a variety of ways, students are drawn in to share their experiences as they relate to this topic.

3. Hear and Enter. Attention turns to the faith story, usually beginning with a Scripture focus and moving to the events and people of the Anabaptist movement. Students are invited to enter into dialogue with the faith story and explore what it has to say to the questions raised by the issue in the earlier steps. The emphasis is to help students discover new insights into the Scriptures.

4. Apply. "So what?" is the question discussed here. How does the Scripture relate to and apply to the issue under consideration?

5. Respond. What are the students willing to do as a result of their study? How will their attitudes and actions be different as a result of this study?

REFLECT AND LOOK AHEAD

Evaluative questions help you reflect on the experience of this session. Here also are reminders of what you need to do for the next session.

DIGGING DEEPER

This section provides background and insights for "Hear and Enter" through additional comments. Read it and let it inspire your teaching.

HANDOUTS

Most sessions include activity handouts that may be photo-copied and distributed to the students.

LEARNING STYLES[1]

Each of us has a special way in which we process or use what we see. This is called our learning style. We learn best when we are taught in ways that complement our learning style.

Where do learning styles come from? Our heredity, past life experiences, the style of a favorite teacher, and the demands of our environment all help create our learning style.

Recent research has shown that there are four main learning styles among North Americans:

•Innovative learners—people who learn by small group interaction and role playing.
•Analytic learners—people who learn through stories and demonstrations.
•Commonsense learners—people who learn by doing.
•Dynamic learners—people who learn by creating.

Effective leaders keep in mind that what is comfortable for them as teachers might not be best for those whose learning styles differ from theirs. No style is right or wrong. We simply learn in different ways. Try to plan at least one activity per session for learners in each of these styles.

[1]The section on learning styles draws from the work of Marlene LeFever in *Creative Teaching Methods* (D.C. Cook, 1985).

SESSION 1
PREPARATION

Scripture text: Galatians 3:10-14

Key verse: No one is justified before God by the law; for "The one who is righteous will live by faith." (Galatians 3:11)

Faith focus: Martin Luther's disagreements with the Roman Catholic church over teachings about how people become right with God helped kick off the Protestant Reformation.

Session goal: To introduce youth to the beginnings of the Protestant Reformation.

A CHANGE IN THE CHURCH

Materials and advance preparation needed:
- Pencils
- Bibles
- Give some thought to appropriate division of roles in the dramatization of Hear and Enter. You may need to assign people to the roles, rather than let them volunteer.
- Small pieces of paper and push pins or scotch tape. Cut two large church doors out of brown construction paper or a cardboard box, and attach them to the bulletin board or wall of your meeting place. (Apply, Option 1)
- Ask someone familiar with the church finances to visit with your youth about your church's budget and offerings. (Apply, Option 2)
- Parents and/or grandparents of some of the youth (Apply, Option 3)

EXPLORATION

Divide the youth into two groups. Ask Group 1: What are some things that would upset you enough to protest against your school? (Possible responses to get them thinking: no lunch break, three hours of math, one minute between classes.) Ask Group 2: What things would upset you enough to protest against your church? (Possible responses: women can't wear pants to church, a three-hour church service.)

FOCUS
(5 minutes)

CONNECT
(5 minutes)

Ask youth to share their answers from Focus. Discuss:
1. How would you protest?
2. How would other people treat you if they disagreed with you?
3. What action would the school take?
4. What action would the church take?

Transition comment: *Today we're going to learn about a man who protested against the church because he felt that the church was not obeying God's Word in some areas that may sound very strange to you.*

HEAR AND ENTER
(20 minutes)

1. Bible Study. Divide youth into groups of three, and give each group a Bible. Ask each group to read Galatians 3:10-14, and to report back what they think the passage is saying. After they have offered their thoughts, add to what they have said, using the following information:

→ The book of Galatians is a letter that the apostle Paul wrote to some churches in Galatia. Paul had started these churches on his first missionary journey. The Jewish Christians were arguing with non-Jewish Christians over whether Christians had to obey all the Jewish laws. In the Bible passage you read, Paul tells the Christians that just obeying the Jewish law was not enough to make people right with God or get them to heaven. In the past, people relied on following the detailed Old Testament law in order to be acceptable to God. But the death and resurrection of Jesus brought a new and better way. The important thing was to have faith in Christ, trusting God to take away our sins and to give us the power to live for God.

Explain to the youth that the man they're going to meet today is Martin Luther, probably the most famous leader of the Protestant Reformation in the 16th century. Luther used this Galatians passage in many of his writings. He taught that "the righteous will live by faith" (Galatians 3:11). Luther understood that people received salvation by putting their faith and trust in Jesus, not by buying God's love through certain acts and rituals. Luther's thinking was quite different from what most people were taught in his day.

2. Dramatic reading. Ask for volunteers, or appoint youth to play the following roles:
• The Roman Catholic church (one person)
• The government (one person)

- Monks and nuns (one or more persons)
- Martin Luther
- The people

Explain that you are going to read about Martin Luther's protest, and when the youth hear their name being read or you pause, they need to act out what is happening. Encourage them to be creative! Your pauses while reading are indicated with a series of periods (...). Here are examples of what youth can do to act out their roles: The Roman Catholic church and the people might cross themselves in the Catholic manner. The person playing the government could flex muscles. Monks and nuns could assume a prayer position, with folded hands and bowed head. Here is the story:

In the 1500s in Europe, the Roman Catholic church ...and the government...worked very closely together. The church was very powerful.... Everyone in Europe belonged to the Roman Catholic church. Its leader, the pope, could influence who would be king or queen for many countries. The church officials had enormous power over many details of people's lives.

It's much, much different today in the Roman Catholic church—and that's another story—but in those days, the government and the Catholic church were so tightly woven together...that even wars were fought in the name of the church. Monks and nuns, this is where you come into the picture.... You were just regular people who got upset that the church had become so worldly...so you gave up your possessions and became monks and nuns.... You dedicated your lives to God, and to prayer....

Martin Luther was one of those people who became a monk.... Luther was a bright man...and a good speaker and debater.... In fact, when he was 26, he was asked to teach at the University of Wittenberg in Wittenberg, Germany....

Luther always thought of God as an angry God, waiting to punish people for sinning....

He struggled with the idea that God is a forgiving God, but one day he read the verse in Galatians that said "the righteous shall live by faith."... LIGHT BULB!...Luther got it! He understood!... God is indeed a forgiving God. People are made right with God by trusting in what God has done, not by anything they do for God.... Luther now had a new direction in his life. He was concerned about the salvation of his fellow church members.

But that's when he ran smack dab into the Roman Catholic church officials....

You see, Catholic people in those days... paid *indulgences*—that's money—to free themselves from sin and to release people from purgatory....

[STOP HERE: Ask the youth if anyone knows what purgatory is. If not, explain that the Catholic church had developed a belief in purgatory as a place where people go after they die, where they are prepared ("purged") to enter either heaven or hell. People believed that you could buy a person out of purgatory by paying money to the church. These sums of money were called indulgences.]

Imagine, Catholic people..., what you would do when your friends and relatives died and the church told you they were in purgatory—but that you could release them and get them on their way to heaven if you just paid an indulgence. What would you do?... But that's not all indulgences could do, the church said. People could pay indulgences to free themselves from sin. What a deal!... Pay money, get forgiveness!...

Martin Luther didn't agree. He told his congregation that God's love was free; people couldn't buy their way into heaven or buy forgiveness from God.... Plus, there was the question of the money from the indulgences. What was happening to it? Any guesses?

[Pause for youth to guess. Ask if they know what the Roman Catholic church officials were doing with the money. If they don't know, or know the partial answer, share the following explanation: Some of the money went to build cathedrals, and some went to pay church officials. Martin Luther was especially upset about one set of indulgences that was raised to help a church leader pay off a loan for the fee he needed to pay to become an archbishop. Most people didn't know where the indulgence money actually went. They didn't know that the Church was becoming increasingly wealthy, and so were the pope, the king, and the other top church officials. Church officials were more interested in money than they were in being servants of Christ. They valued people for their money, not for who they were.]

Luther was angry with the corruption he saw.... To make his opinions known, Luther wrote 95 statements on paper.... He wanted to debate these statements with the church officials.

As a way to get their attention, late at night on October 31, 1517, Luther nailed the statements on the church door. (The door served as the town bulletin board.)... The statements are known as the Ninety-five Theses.

October 31 is now called Reformation Day because Luther wanted to reform, or change some of the church's way of thinking. But at that time, the Roman Catholic church didn't want to change its ways. Church officials were outraged with Luther.... After four years of debate, they asked Luther to take back his writings.... Luther said, "Unless I am convinced by Scripture and plain reason [ask youth to repeat each part of the statement after you], ...I do not accept the authority of the popes and councils...for they have contradicted each other.... My conscience is captive to the Word of God.... I cannot and I will not recant anything...for to go against conscience is neither right nor safe.... God help me.... Amen."

Luther was thrown out of the church.... He was considered an outlaw and his life was in danger. His friends kidnapped him and kept him safely hidden.... The Protestant Reformation had begun—the reformation based on a protest.

[Applaud the youth and tell them they did a great job!]

3. Discussion: Was Martin Luther right to criticize the church? Why or why not? What do you think about the idea of "buying your way" out of sin? Should we criticize our church today? If we have a complaint, who should we talk to?

Ask the youth: *Are you a Protestant? Stand up if you are.* Youth may not know whether they are, and this is a good time to let them know this is the history of our church and our denomination that we're talking about. The question is one they may want to ask themselves at different points of the study.

APPLY
(10 minutes)

Option 1: Hand out small pieces of paper and pencils to each youth. Ask them to make two columns: "Change " and "Same, " and to write things about the church that they would like to see changed, and things they would like to keep the same. When they are finished, "nail" the papers on the church doors you made on the bulletin board or wall. Read and discuss them. (Note: You may want to give these notes to your pastor or someone in church leadership who would like to know what some of the youth are thinking about the church.)

Option 2: Invite someone from your congregation to come talk to the youth about the church finances. Tell the youth that while the Catholic church during Martin Luther's time used indulgences to finance the church, we give offerings to the church to support it. Although the way the church gets the money is different, there is discussion today just like there was then about how the money is to be used and the attitudes with which people give.

Some possible questions for the person you invite: How much money does it take to run the church? How is the money divided? Are there church dues? Is there a set rate? If so, how is the rate determined? Besides the operation of the church, what other areas do our offerings go to?

Option 3: Invite parents and/or grandparents of the youth to the class to share how the church has changed during their lifetimes. Discuss those changes with the youth. How important are the changes? Is change always uncomfortable? Is it good or bad?

RESPOND
(5 minutes)

- If you did Option 1 in Apply, ask each youth to pray about either their "Same" or their "Change" suggestion. This prayer can be done in a non-threatening, conversational manner, as if they are talking to God in the room. You should lead by example, then go around the room.
- If you did Option 2 or 3, have the youth come up with one thing they would seriously like to see changed in the congregation or the larger church denomination—something they feel would help them grow closer to God or would help others in the church. Decide how you might share that information with people who make decisions—through a letter or a personal visit, perhaps. Close with a prayer for your church.

REFLECT
Did the youth understand the concepts of purgatory and indulgences? Did they understand what made Martin Luther disagree with these issues enough to protest publicly? Did they understand the importance

and workings of their church? Are the youth making the connection of what happened hundreds of years ago, to their own lives and church today?

DIGGING DEEPER

On a hot summer day in July, 1505, a young student named Martin Luther was walking to a village in the German region of Saxony. A thunderstorm came up, and out of it, a bolt of lightning struck, knocking Luther to the ground. Terrified, he cried out "St. Anne, help me! I will become a monk!"

Much to his parents' disappointment, who wanted him to practice law, Luther did enter a monastery that year. As a monk, he studied, prayed, worked, and sought peace for his soul, but he couldn't quite accept the idea of grace—the love and forgiveness that comes to us no matter what we've done. He saw God as an angry God, not a loving parent.

Luther became a professor at the University of Wittenberg. One day as he prepared his lectures, a verse in Romans seemed to jump out at him. "The one who is righteous will live by faith." He was familiar with similar passages in Romans but never before had they impacted him as they did that day. That day, he knew that Christian faith was all about grace—that no amount of works will redeem us. Only God's free grace and Christ's love could. Luther felt free and forgiven for the first time, and his life took on new meaning.

About that time, there was a vacancy in the archbishopric of Mainz. This large region would mean a large income for the person who became the archbishop. The Catholic church offered the job to Albert of Brandenburg but he would have to pay his installation fee, set at twelve thousand *ducants*—"for the twelve apostles," he was told.

Albert counter-offered seven thousand, supposedly for the seven deadly sins, and in the end they settled on ten thousand. Albert borrowed the money. Then, to raise the money to pay the loan, the pope permitted the proclamation of an indulgence. Half of the proceeds would go to Albert, (unbeknownst to the person paying the indulgence), and the other half would help construct St. Peter's Cathedral in Rome. The indulgence seller traveled throughout Germany, promising that as soon as the money hit the box, the donor's relatives and friends would be released from purgatory.

Martin Luther, who had gone through such agony to find salvation, was not impressed, to say the least. In response, he walked to the Castle Church in

Wittenberg on the last day of October, 1517, and fastened ninety-five theses or statements to the door. The theses were written in Latin and stated that the grace of God, not human works, forgives sins and reconciles us to God. Some statements criticized the pope. Students quickly translated the theses into German, and soon Luther became known throughout Germany and beyond. The Protestant Reformation was begun.

(Based on *Through Fire and Water*, pages 59-74. See page 65 for examples of the Ninety-five Theses.)

SESSION 2
PREPARATION

Scripture: Matthew 22:29

Key verse: You know neither the scriptures nor the power of God. (Matthew 22:29)

Faith focus: Conrad Grebel, Felix Manz, and George Blaurock studied the Bible and their lives were changed dramatically as a result.

Session goal: Introduce youth to three important leaders in the Anabaptist movement, and help them see the importance of studying the Bible.

THREE MEN AND A BIBLE

Materials and advance preparation needed:
- Bibles
- Handout for "To Tell the Truth," including the Beatitudes from Eugene Peterson's *The Message*
- Optional but encouraged: Hang up posters of Conrad Grebel, Felix Manz, and George Blaurock (sold separately as companions to this study guide; see Introduction, p. 5-6)

EXPLORATION

"Big Impression Charades"
Ask youth to think of a book, movie, or person who has made a big impression in their life. Then play charades, taking turns acting out and guessing what it is. Let the youth use sounds as well as motions if that helps.

FOCUS
(10 minutes)

Say: *We all have things and people who have made big impressions on us and influenced our lives. Today we are going to meet three men whose lives were changed dramatically, thanks to a very important book. The way we are going to meet them is through the game "To Tell the Truth."* If you have not ordered the color posters of Conrad Grebel, Felix Manz, and George Blaurock for your classroom, pictures of them are included on page 23.

CONNECT
(5 minutes)

HEAR AND ENTER
(20 minutes)

1. To Tell the Truth. Distribute the handout and play the game. You will need three people who will leave the room and decide which one of them is the real Conrad Grebel, and which are imposters. They will have the same information sheets that the class members will have. Allow time for them and the rest of the group to read the profiles on the sheets before they are called back in.

When they return, instruct the youth to ask "Conrad Grebel #1" a question, then #2, and so on, until you feel it's time to have the "Real Conrad Grebel stand up." Continue the game the same way with Felix Manz and George Blaurock, using different sets of youth. Be prepared to help with some questions yourself if needed. They could include:
1. Tell me about your family.
2. Where were you educated?
3. Have you ever done anything that got you in trouble? What was it?
4. Have you ever been in jail?

At some point, you may wish to point out Felix Manz' hymn "I Sing with Exultation," in *Hymnal: A Worship Book* (438).

2. Discussion. Ask the youth which book all three of these men had in common. (A strong commitment to Bible study.) What difference did it make in their lives?

APPLY
(10 minutes)

Draw the group's attention to the handout's Beatitudes quote from *The Message* by Eugene Peterson. Put youth in pairs, and assign each pair two Beatitudes, asking them to come up with a quick demonstration that would illustrate the Beatitides. (It doesn't have to be something that has happened to them, but it should be something that relates to youth their age.)

When they are done, compliment them on a good job, and then say: *You know, the cool thing about the Bible is that it was a life-changing book for Conrad, Felix, and George in the 1500s, and it is still a life-changing book today. The Bible teaches us about God, how to relate to God, and how to follow Jesus as our Savior and Lord. There's a story in Matthew about Jesus talking to the Sadducees who were arguing about something, and his answer was "You are wrong, because you know neither the Scriptures nor the power of God." Jesus was saying that we need to study the Scriptures so we know how to live and how to relate to each other. It is through the Bible that God communicates with us.*

Ask someone to read verses 10, 11, 12 from Matthew 5. Then say: *Keep these verses in mind, because they will become very important as we continue our study of Anabaptists.*

RESPOND
(5 minutes)

Ask youth to turn to the Beatitudes in their Bibles (Matt. 5:3-12) and to pick out one that they are willing to pray about and to try to work on in the coming week. Allow some silent time for them to do this, then close with prayer, asking God to be with them in the coming week.

REFLECT

Did the youth see the differences in the three men? Did they see how the Bible was an important part of their lives and how they changed as a result of studying it? Do they know how important the Bible is in shaping our commitment to God?

DIGGING DEEPER

In the last session, we met Martin Luther, who was a leader in the Reformation in Germany. Besides emphasizing salvation by faith (see last session), Luther was known and persecuted for emphasizing the authority of the Bible, rather than church tradition.

Quite independent of Luther but influenced by his writings was Ulrich Zwlingli of Switzerland. Although Zwingli and Luther agreed on the need for reform, they differed in one very important area: Luther argued that Christ was bodily present in the bread and wine of communion, and Zwlingli maintained that it was Christ's spiritual presence in communion but not his body.

In 1525 the Reformation in Switzerland was well under way, with Zwingli speaking out against the Roman church's practices and beliefs relating to monastic vows, clerical celibacy, purgatory, praying to saints, treating Catholic mass as a sacrifice, and teaching that salvation can be earned by doing good works. As he preached from the Bible, Zwingli criticized abuses in the church, and took decisive action in reforming the church.

He was supported by the city council of Zurich. The city authorities did, however, warn him not to proceed too rapidly lest the common people find the changes too radical and too swift. Like Luther in Germany, Zwingli didn't want to alienate the people or oppose the council.

Not so with several of his young followers. Conrad Grebel, Felix Manz, and George Blaurock felt that the reforms weren't happening fast enough, and criticized Zwingli for always checking with "my lords" on matters that pertained to the church and faith. They believed that only the Word of God should be consulted and then acted upon promptly. Studying the Bible had turned their lives around, and they were preaching and teaching that the Word of God, not the city magistrates, should govern the spiritual lives of the people. (For more, see *Through Fire and Water*, pages 82-85.)

HANDOUT
To Tell the Truth and the Beatitudes

Conrad Grebel

Felix Manz

George Blaurock

Profiles for
"To Tell the Truth"

Conrad Grebel

I was born to a wealthy family in Zurich, Switzerland. My family was well known in Zurich. My father was on the City Council—a very prestigious position.

I had the opportunity to go to the best schools. I traveled to other countries to go to college. I went to the University of Basel for one year. Then I received a grant from the King of Austria, so I went to the University of Vienna. Vienna was known for its wealth and beauty and I got caught up in the city life. My education didn't seem too important to me anymore. All I wanted to do was go to parties and get drunk.

At that time, fighting was common among the college students. Unfortunately, I got into many fights with other students. In one fight, I almost lost my hand.

After three years in Vienna I got a scholarship from the King of France. I went to the University of Paris. But there I got into another fight and two men were killed. I was told to leave the college. I had been in Paris for only three months.

I didn't know what to do, so I went back home to Zurich. My father was not pleased. My allowance was cut off. I had no money and no job. Two years later, I got married and we lived with my parents. My situation was awful and, I admit, I complained quite a bit. My health wasn't good, my family wasn't getting along, and I still didn't have a job.

Then I met Ulrich Zwingli, a priest in the Grossmunster Church in Zurich. I already knew how to speak Latin, and German was my native language. Now I began to study Hebrew and Greek with Zwingli. Zwingli gave me the Bible to study. I learned how God wanted people to act and I knew my way of life needed to change. I became a Christian.

Felix Manz

My father was a Roman Catholic Church priest. I got a good education in Zurich and later at the University of Paris. I was known as a scholar in Hebrew. I could also read and speak Latin and Greek.

When I met Ulrich Zwingli, he encouraged me to study the Bible as he did with Conrad Grebel. He wanted me to teach at a university, but I became too involved with following Jesus. I baptized many people and I preached God's Word.

The government told me to quit preaching or I would be thrown in jail. I did not stop preaching or baptizing others, so I got thrown in jail. Jail time is no fun, but I spent most of my time praying. I prayed for God to give me the strength to face my future. I prayed that God would use me as his witness. I also wrote a song titled "I Sing with Exultation."

While in jail, I was interrogated by the Zurich city council members. They wanted to know why I believed like I did, whom I had baptized, and where I baptized them. I wouldn't answer.

These council members tried to get me to change my mind and see their point of view, but I wouldn't. I knew what the Bible taught and I believed the Bible. I would rather sit in jail than go against God's Word.

George Blaurock

I was a priest in the Roman Catholic Church before I met Ulrich Zwingli. Ulrich gave me the Bible to study, like he did with Conrad and Felix. I studied the Bible and understood the importance of God's Word. I was so excited about what I read and learned that I couldn't wait to tell others. My life sure changed. And I guess you could say I wasn't exactly shy about this change in my life.

For example, one Sunday morning I went to a state-run church. The pastor had just stepped in the pulpit to preach, when I stood up and asked him what he intended to do.

"Preach the Word of God," he answered.

I told him that I was called to preach, but no one would let me. I was pretty persistent, and finally a deputy told me to keep quiet or I would be arrested. I decided to keep quiet. I didn't really want to cause trouble; I only wanted every person in the congregation to understand what the Bible taught.

Some people have nicknamed me "Strong George" because I'm tall and I have a strong faith. It seems I get nickmaned a lot. Even the name "Blaurock" is a German nickname meaning blue (<u>blau</u>) coat (<u>Rock</u>). You guessed it... I almost always wear a blue jacket. But my legal full name is George Cajacob.

The Beatitudes

You're blessed when you're at the end of your rope. With less of you there is more of God and his rule.

You're blessed when you feel you've lost what is most dear to you. Only then can you be embraced by the One most dear to you.

You're blessed when you're content with just who you are—no more, no less. That's the moment you find yourselves proud owners of everything that can't be bought.

You're blessed when you've worked up a good appetite for God. He's food and drink in the best meal you'll ever eat.

You're blessed when you care. At the moment of being "care-full," you find yourselves cared for.

You 're blessed when you get your inside world—your mind and heart—put right. Then you can see God in the outside world.

You're blessed when you can show people how to cooperate instead of compete or fight. That's when you discover who you really are, and your place in God's family.

You're blessed when your commitment to God provokes persecution. The persecution drives you even deeper into God's kingdom.

Count yourselves blessed every time people put you down or throw you out or speak lies about you to discredit me. . . . You can be glad when that happens—give a cheer, even!—for though they don't like it, I do!

(Matthew 5:3-12 from *The Message*, by Eugene Peterson, NavPress, 1993, page 18. Used with permission)

SESSION 3

PREPARATION

Scripture text: Joshua 24:14-15

Key verse: Choose this day whom you will serve…but as for me and my household, we will serve the LORD. (Joshua 24:15)

Faith focus: Joshua and the Israelites, Conrad Grebel and Ulrich Zwingli, and each of us today—we all must choose whom we will worship and obey.

Session goal: Help youth to think about the decisions they make, particularly those that are related to God and following Jesus.

> **Materials and advance preparation needed:**
> - Handouts copied for the Grebels, Zwinglis, and City Council
> - Questions on pieces of paper (see Apply), and a hat in which to put them

EXPLORATION

Ask the youth to stand together in the center of the room. Read the following sets of words, one at a time, asking youth to move to one side of the room if they like the first word in the set, and the other side of the room if they prefer the second option. Feel free to add more to the list or change it if you wish.

FOCUS
(5 minutes)

vanilla/chocolate ice cream
candy bar/chips
music/sports
math/history
cleaning house/baby-sitting
dogs/cats
lake/mountains

After the youth have returned to their seats, ask:
1. *Was one choice better than another?*
2. *Why is it important to have choices? Or is it important?*
3. *What choices do you make in your everyday lives?*

CONNECT
(5 minutes)

(Examples: what to wear; whether to do homework or watch TV; how to relate to family and friends)

4. *Does God let us choose whether or not we want to be followers of Jesus? Why? Why doesn't God just make it automatic for us?*

Transition comment: *Today we're going to talk about choices. In the Scripture passage today, the Israelites had to choose whether they would worship God or idols. Those who were part of the Anabaptist movement also had to choose whom they would obey.*

HEAR AND ENTER
(20 minutes)

1. Bible study. Ask a student to read Joshua 24: 14-15.

2. Connect the Bible passage to today's story. Say something like: *Joshua called the tribes of Israel together and reminded them of how God had led them out of Egypt, through the parted Red Sea, and across the desert. He reminded the people of the many miracles God had performed for them. After those reminders of how good God had been to them, Joshua encouraged the Israelites to remain faithful to God. The people promised they would worship only God and not any idols. Joshua took a large stone and set it up under a tree so the Israelites would always remember their promise.*

The Israelites had to choose whether to obey God. Now we're going to look at the choices that one young man wanted to be available for Christian people and the church in the 16th century. Around the time that Martin Luther nailed his 95 statements to the door in Wittenburg, Germany, Conrad Grebel—one of the men we met briefly in the last session—was asking some of the same questions about the church. In Zurich, Switzerland, there was also a lot of discussion about change in the Catholic church. As we saw last time, a man named Ulrich Zwingli also wanted to reform the church, and convinced the City Council to bring about some changes. But Conrad Grebel, Felix Manz, George Blaurock and others felt that Zwingli wasn't going far enough. A big question was how much freedom church people should have to choose for themselves what to believe.

3. Debate. Divide the class into three groups: The Zwlinglis , the Grebels, and the Zurich City Council. Give each group a copy of the information about themselves to read and study. The Zwinglis and the Grebels are to prepare a debate to present to the Council, trying to convince it of their viewpont. The Council should come up with questions to ask both sides. Give the groups 5 to 10 minutes to prepare, then start the debate. As moderator, be sure to keep control over who has the floor. After 10 minutes of debating, bring it to a close. There is no need to determine who "won."

4. Discuss:
1. Why did Conrad Grebel 's father vote against Conrad?
2. What are the pros and cons of a church being tied in with the government?
3. Why would the law state that only pastors could teach the Bible?
4. If churches were still run by the government, how might our church be different?
5. What does today's story mean for you and your church?

In Conrad Grebel's time, the state church had a great deal of control over how people interpreted the Bible. The Bibles were written in Latin, and most people couldn't read them. The Bibles were also chained to the pulpits, so people couldn't get to them. The church thought that is was dangerous for people to read and interpret the Bible themselves. Who knows what ideas they would come up with on their own! So the Church interpreted the Bible and told the people how to live. Conrad Grebel believed differently. He believed people should study the Bible together and be free to choose how they lived out its teachings.

APPLY
(10 minutes)

Say: *The choices you make every day may not seem as big as the ones we talked about today, but they are very important. Pick a question out of the hat and share your answer with the group. Put the question back in the hat when you're done. It's okay for several people to get the same question.*
Questions to have on slips of paper in hat:
- Tell us about a decision you made this week.
- Why did you choose to come to church today?
- How much freedom do you have in making choices that affect you?
- How much freedom do you think you should have in making choices?
- Who do you depend on the most to help you make decisions?
- If you could choose whether or not to come to church, what would you choose?
- What is one of the biggest decisions you've made in your life so far?

- What is a decision your parent or another adult made that affected you?
- What is a decision you've made that has affected someone else?
- What is a decision you will have to make in the future that has you worried?
- What is a decision you are looking forward to making in the future?
- Do you think God can help you make decisions? How?

For the closing prayer time, you may want to make some discreet notes as they are sharing.

RESPOND
(5 minutes)

Close the class with prayer, thanking God for our freedom to make choices and decisions. If you can, pray specifically for each student in the class and something he or she said about their decisions.

REFLECT

Did the youth grasp how Conrad Grebel rocked the city of Zurich by speaking against the church? Are they appreciating the fact that they can freely study the Bible because of what their forebears did? Did they make the connection between the decisions that these men made and the everyday decisions they make?

DIGGING DEEPER

As we learned in the last session, a significant rift began to develop between the reformer, Ulrich Zwlingli, and several of his followers. Zwingli's way of dealing with matters of reform and disagreement was to hold debates in which the reformers, the city leaders, and the people participated. These debates were often a farce, however, because Zwingli had the magistrates in his back pocket and he was always declared the winner, and his opponents were the losers. This involvement of the magistrates in spiritual matters made it even more obvious to Grebel and the other radicals that the church and state needed to be separated.

Who were these radicals? For one thing, they were young. Conrad Grebel and Felix Manz, for example, died before the age of 30; and they are now recognized as founders of the Anabaptist movement. Secondly, they felt so strongly about their beliefs that they faced repeated arrest, imprisonment, and possible death. They were not deterred in their zeal to preach and baptize new believers. This combination of youth and enthusiasm probably gave these men the ideals, courage, and energy for radical action that may not have been as easy for older people who may have been more cautious and practical.

Also, as we see in the records of the debates and in the letters some of the Anabaptist radicals wrote to Luther and another German reformer, Thomas Muentzer—these young adults weren't afraid to dialogue and tangle with the leaders of the Reformation. In one example, Conrad Grebel wrote Martin Luther, challenging him not to use the weakness of Christians as an excuse for not working more courageously toward reform. According to Grebel, Luther, like Zwingli, was more concerned with pleasing people than following the Word of God. It seems that Luther never responded to Grebel's letter, but that someone in Wittenberg learned that Luther didn't know how to answer Grebel. Before long, in fact, Luther was among those who were persecuting the Anabaptists. (*Through Fire and Water*, pages 85-93)

HANDOUTS
The Zwinglis
The Grebels
The Zurich City Council

The Zwinglis

You are all Ulrich Zwinglis. You are a very smart man, and not just because you are a scholar. You know how to get your way. You knew how to achieve your goal of a reformed church. Over time, you had the Zurich City Council agreeing to whatever changes in the church you wanted. Eventually you even got the okay to allow all priests to preach from the Bible.

You argue against purgatory, celibacy (singleness) of ministers, prayer to saints, and transubstantiation (in communion, the belief that the bread and wine literally change into Christ's body and blood). You believe that the Bible is the ultimate authority in the church and that Christ is the head of the church. But you also believe in infant baptism, and you want to keep the church and the government tightly knit. Thanks to that partnership between the church and government, the Reformation in Switzerland is humming right along.

You believe God is on your side. After all, you have been studying the New Testament and preaching what Jesus taught. You are a powerful preacher and many people are hearing you and agreeing with your views. Thanks to this following and the cooperation of the government, the Reformed Church has been successful.

Your friend Conrad Grebel—he's got some weird ideas in his head. For one, he won't baptize his infant son, putting him in danger of eternal hell. What kind of man would do that? Why in the world wouldn't a person want his children to be baptized into the church?

The other thing about Conrad is that he's just too pushy. He wants things done right now, and doesn't understand that sometimes it takes time to work the system. He wants the church and government to be separated. "A house divided can't stand" is your philosophy. If the Reformed Church is going to be successful, you need the government behind you, not against you. Conrad is just overanxious.

In fact, he's done the unthinkable and split off from you. You were best of friends in this Reformation thing and now he's split to do his own thing, and he has taken some of your followers with him. Division and dissension are not good, so you went to talk to him and tried to convince him to come back. But NO! Stubborn old guy. He wouldn't do it. So now it's come to a debate in front of the City Council. How embarrassing for Conrad's own father, who's on the Council. You're sure glad you have friends on the Council.

The Grebels

Your are all Conrad Grebels. Remember, you were born into a wealthy family in Zurich, Switzerland. You studied in several universities, then returned to your hometown of Zurich, got married and tried to find a job. Then you met Ulrich Zwingli—a guy about your age who was all excited about making some changes in the Roman Catholic church. While Luther has been in Germany, challenging the Roman Catholic church, Zwingli has been asking questions of the church in Switzerland.

You and Zwingli became good friends. You were excited about what Zwingli was teaching. But after three years of getting along, you are now having a major disagreement. Here's the problem: Zwingli keeps running to the City Council with church matters. You want a church free from the government's authority.

And there's another thing: The church has always baptized babies. Until now, as soon as an infant is baptized, he or she has automatically joined the church. From your study of the Bible you believe that a person must be able to have faith in God and make a commitment to follow Christ before being baptized. A baby doesn't have faith yet. At baptism, a baby can't make the decision to follow Christ. To make that point, you and your wife refused to have your baby son baptized, and this has enraged members of the Council.

You believe that a church should be made up of believers in God who commit their lives to following Christ, are baptized as adults, and voluntarily join the church.. You want people to have the freedom to choose what church they belong to, to choose to follow Christ, to choose to worship God, to choose to study the Bible whenever and wherever they want to.

You are also frustrated with Zwingli because he's so cautious and slow about the changes in the church. For example, when the City Council said no to changes the first time, he was willing to wait. You wanted changes to happen NOW! In fact, you and Felix Manz told Zwingli that you want to create a new church that believes differently than the Roman Catholic church or Zwingli's Reformed Church. This new church would elect a new City Council who would be more fair and would listen to what you believe and let you have a church separate from the government.

But Zwingli didn't help you. You and Zwingli went your separate ways. Felix Manz went with you, and some other Zwingli followers followed you too. Zwingli came back begging, but you said "No way." But it isn't that easy. Because the church and government are still officially all wrapped up together, you can't just leave. The government won't allow it. So a debate has been scheduled for January 25 in front of the City Council. It's you versus your former friend Zwingli, debating your belief about church. To make matters more complicated, your own father is on the Council.

The Zurich City Council

You are the governing body of Zurich, and one of you is the father of Conrad Grebel. You are going to hear the debate between Conrad Grebel and Ulrich Zwingli regarding the involvement of the church and government and this disagreement about baptizing babies. The truth is, you know who is going to win the debate because you know whose side you are on. You are backing Ulrich Zwingli. (Tough luck for Conrad's father.)

Although you know who will win this debate, you must act as though you are listening to both sides. You will ask two basic questions of both men: 1) Tell us what you believe about infant baptism and why. 2) Tell us what you believe about how closely the church and government should be tied together, and why.

Once you have asked the questions and heard the answers, you will discuss among yourselves who is the winner of the debate and what the results will be. You will declare Ulrich Zwingli to be in the right and Conrad Grebel to be in the wrong. You will tell Conrad that a new set of laws has been enacted, and that all parents must have their babies baptized by the time they are eight days old, or the family will be thrown out of Zurich. You will tell Conrad Grebel that he and his followers have one week to baptize their babies or they will be thrown out of town, and that he can no longer hold Bible meetings. End of council session.

SESSION 4
PREPARATION

THE REBAPTIZERS

Scripture text: Matthew 28: 16-20

Key verse: Make disciples of all nations, baptizing them...and teaching them to obey everything that I have commanded you. (Matthew 28:19-20)

Faith focus: Anabaptists believe that people should be baptized when they are old enough to understand the commitment involved in following Christ.

Session goal: To help youth understand what the Anabaptists believed about baptism, and to think about their beliefs.

Materials and advance preparation needed:
- Basin of water, towel (Focus)
- Pencils
- Bed or sofa for drama in Hear and Enter
- Optional: Little prizes for the quiz in Hear and Enter
- Appoint readers for the drama in Hear and Enter and practice ahead of time, if possible.
- If the youth take you up on Option 3 in Apply, be prepared to tell your own story of a time when you stood up for your beliefs, your baptism, and anything else the youth might ask.
- Optional snacks for Respond "party"
- Copies of the two handouts

EXPLORATION

Pass a basin of water around the group, asking students to dip their hands in the water and say what comes to mind when they feel the water. What do they associate with water?

FOCUS
(5 minutes)

Ask:
1. *What happens in church that is water-related?*
2. *How does baptism happen?*
3. *Who is baptized?*
4. *When are people baptized?*

CONNECT
(5 minutes)

5. Where does it happen?
6. Why do people get baptized?

HEAR AND ENTER (20 minutes)	1. Read Matthew 28:16-20 aloud. 2. Connect the Bible passage to today's story by saying: *The Bible verses today are sometimes called Jesus' Great Commission. Jesus had already been crucified and he had risen from the grave. Right before he ascended into heaven Jesus talked with the disciples and gave them a task. He "commissioned" them to go into the world, spread God's Word, make more disciples, and baptize them. In today's drama, you will find out how Conrad Grebel and the earliest Anabaptists felt about the issue of baptism and what they did about spreading God's Word. Warning: there will be a pop quiz at the end, so listen closely!* 3. Assign roles and read through the drama "Danger: Baptism." 4. Hand out the quiz "All Shook Up" and ask everyone to write brief answers. When they are done, go through it together. Find out if anyone got all of the answers right. Optional: give prizes to the ones who scored high on the quiz.
APPLY (10 mintues)	**O**ption 1: Tell your own story of a time when you had to stand up for your beliefs. Ask students if they have stories to share about a time when they stood up for something they believed in. **O**ption 2: Invite several adults (could be parents or grandparents of the youth) to the class to talk about what their baptism meant to them—when it happened, how old they were, how the decided, etc. **O**ption 3: Tell the class that it isn't really fair for you to give them a quiz and to ask them questions all the time. Invite the class to get together and come up with a quiz for you about this session! (Good luck!)
RESPOND	Do a time-travel exercise. Say: *Imagine it is 10 years from now. We have all gathered together to celebrate the fact that we had this lesson on (say today's day and year). I know it seems silly, but play along with me, okay? We are going to celebrate and reminisce with each other about the difference this lesson made in our lives. Think about it, imagine what it could possibly have to do with your future.*

Optional: Share snacks and make this a "party."

REFLECT AND LOOK AHEAD

Were the youth able to understand the risk Conrad Grebel and his group were taking by being baptized as adults? Did they understand baptism and what it means? Which members of the group are thinking about declaring their own commitment to Christ by being baptized? Make a point of encouraging them individually sometime soon.

The next session is about the tremendous price thousands of Anabaptists paid for their faith. The story is about Anabaptist martyrs, and it would be good for you to take a copy of *Martyrs Mirror* to class so the youth get an idea of how many stories there actually are. Also, one of the options includes reading or telling a story from *On Fire for Christ*. This book retells stories of Anabaptist martyrs in a context that is easy to read and understand.

DIGGING DEEPER

Read

The debate about infant and adult (or believer's) baptism was of great importance for the Reformation movement and the emergence of the Anabaptists. Conrad Grebel, Felix Manz, George Blaurock, and others in their group in Zurich were somewhat influenced by other radical reformers in Germany, including Thomas Muentzer and Andrew Carlstadt. As they read their writings, and especially as they studied the New Testament themselves, the radicals became convinced that there was no biblical basis for baptizing infants.

Grebel and the Zurich radicals decided not to baptize their own children. However, after the debate of January 17, 1525, Zwingi and the City Council decided that all infants must be baptized and that adult rebaptism was not acceptable. A few days later, Conrad Grebel and his friends performed the first believer's baptism among themselves. This was to become a repeated pattern across Europe. Those who had been baptized as infants now asked to be baptized upon their personal declaration of faith. Naturally, they were called Anabaptists—the rebaptizers.

For the Anabaptists faith had to come before baptism, following the words of Jesus in Mark 16:16: "The one who believes and is baptized will be saved." Since infants cannot testify to a conscious faith, the Anabaptists believed they shouldn't be baptized. When they become teenagers or adults, however, they are capable of making personal life decisions, such as the choice to follow Christ. Some Anabaptists went so far as to ridicule infant baptism as "a dog's bath." Obviously, this didn't sit very well with the Catholic and Protestant society in which they were living.

Why was baptism such a big deal? Because at that time, most people believed that baptism not only removed sin from the baby, but also made the baby a member of the church. To postpone baptism would divide society into Christians and non-Christians. For Zwingli and other mainline reformers, adult baptism would result in a large part of society remaining pagan. Zwingli believed in a Christian society where all were baptized believers and were part of the church.

The Anabaptists, on the other hand, believed that faith was to be received voluntarily. Baptism and church membership were only for those who repented of their sins and made a personal decision to follow Jesus. Anabaptists believed that unbaptized children were safe in Christ and thus could wait until they were old enough and able to respond to God's grace. When the Radicals practiced their beliefs on baptism, they became targets of hatred from the rest of society.

(*Through Fire and Water*, pages 86-87)

HANDOUTS
Danger: Baptism
All Shook Up

DANGER: Baptism
a drama

Characters:
Conrad Grebel
George Blaurock
Four friends of Grebel
Narrator

Conrad Grebel is lying down. The others are gathered around him.

Conrad: (*weakly*) It's kind of you to come see me.

George: Hey, we miss you, man.

Friend 1: We've been praying for you, and we had to come see how you're doing.

Conrad: Not so good, I'm afraid.

Friend 2: You'll get better, brother Conrad. We're praying really hard. Surely God knows how much our movement needs your leadership.

George: That's so true! Remember that meeting when you baptized me?

Conrad: How could I forget? We weren't supposed to be meeting. If the authorities found out, they were going to throw us in jail. We wanted to meet to read the Bible and pray, but that was against the law.

Friend 3: We met at Felix Manz' house because we thought they wouldn't look for us there.

Friend 4: I'll never forget how we read Acts 5. And when verse 29 said "We must obey God rather than any human authority," Conrad yelled out, "There it is! We must obey God, not the government!"

George: That's when I knew what I wanted to do. I knelt in front of you, brother Conrad, and asked you to baptize me.

Conrad: I didn't want to do it. It was against the law. Even though I'd just read that verse, I was scared of being arrested, thrown in jail, or killed.

George: But I insisted. My baptism as an infant was meaningless to me. I wanted to be baptized because of my faith in Jesus and my commitment to him.

Friend 1: You said, "This could get us killed."

Conrad: George was kneeling in front of me. I took the water dipper and poured some water on his head, saying "I baptize you in the name of the Father, the Son, and the Holy Spirit. May the Lord baptize you with his Spirit from above."

Friend 2: After that, we all got in line. We all wanted to be baptized.

Friend 3: We were scared and excited all at the same time. But mostly, we felt God's presence there in that house like we'd never felt before. I'll never forget it.

Friend 4: Me neither.

George: We talked about what we should call our group, and we decided on "The Swiss Brethren." But that's not what people called us.

Conrad: (*laughs weakly*): No, they have their own name for us. The Anabaptists. The rebaptizers.

Friend 4: You must be getting tired, Conrad. We'll leave you now. Get some rest, and we'll be back soon. Our prayers are with you.

Narrator: The Anabaptist movement began in Zurich, Switzerland in 1525, and Conrad Grebel was a very important leader in it. Unfortunately, he died of the plague when he was just 28 years old, only 18 months after the movement began.

All Shook Up

Quiz

1. What book of the Bible was the believer reading from at the meeting we witnessed?

2. BONUS: Write the verse that helped the group decide what to do.

3. What did the group call themselves?

4. What did other people call the group? Why?

5. In which country did the Anabaptist movement start?

6. Which year did it begin?

7. Are you an Anabaptist?

8. Read the following and answer the questions at the end:

Think about what Conrad Grebel did and why the government was shaken up. The government and the church were always linked together. The people didn't know any other arrangement (just like we today can hardly imagine the government and church *not* being separate).

   As we saw in an earlier session, Martin Luther rocked the boat. He challenged the church's authority by saying that indulgences and other practices in the church were wrong . Ulrich Zwingli and other leaders in Zurich agreed with Luther and joined the reform movement. Then Conrad Grebel came along and studied the Bible by himself, along with his little group of radicals. Grebel went further than Luther and Zwingli by questioning beliefs that the Reformers did not question, such as infant baptism and the joining together of the church and the state.

   The government rulers didn't want these views to spread. The Anabaptists posed a huge threat to the authority of the church and the government. The rulers saw their orderly world of one church and one government falling apart. These Anabaptists had to be stopped, the rulers thought, before their entire way of life would be changed.

• When have you felt shaken you up by realizing that something you always believed was wrong?
• How did you react?
• Do you think the people in your church are as strong in their beliefs as those first Anabaptists were? Why or why not?

SESSION 5
PREPARATION

Scripture text: Matthew 5:10-12

Key Verse: Blessed are those who are persecuted for righteousness' sake, for theirs is the kingdom of heaven. (Matthew 5:10)

Faith focus: The Anabaptist martyrs paid a high price for their faith, but they were willing to suffer torture and death because they knew God was with them.

Session goal: Help youth realize that for the Anabaptists, and for Christians today, being persecuted and killed for their faith is a horrible thing to experience, but God is with them in those tough times.

BLESSED ARE THE PICKED ON

Materials and advance preparation needed:
- Copy of *Martyrs Mirror*
- Enough sharp screws for each student and two six-foot lengths of rope
- Four copies of the skit, "Standing Up to Death." Ideally, it would be good to involve four adults from the church to prepare this skit prior to class and have them present it to the youth. If not, have youth from within the class help you present it.
- Copies of the handout "About Those Women"
- Optional activity in Hear and Enter: story from the book *On Fire for Christ*.
- Someone to share with the class about being persecuted for their faith (Option 2, Apply)

EXPLORATION

Option 1: Ask students to tell about a time they were picked on. What happened? How did it feel?

Option 2: Ask for volunteers who are willing to be "picked on." Then, as a class, find something about the students to make fun of, but make sure this is done so that there are not hurt feelings. For example, pick on the person for wearing brown shoes, or something that isn't at all personal. Exaggerate and have fun, and then immediately process how it felt to be the brunt of the harassment.

FOCUS
(5 minutes)

CONNECT

Say: *We've talked about being picked on, which actually is a type of torture and persecution. Today we're going to find out what Jesus said about being tortured and persecuted, and what happened to some of the Anabaptists.*

HEAR AND ENTER
(25 minutes)

1. Read Matthew 5:1-12 aloud together. As you read, ask them to listen carefully for anything Jesus says that relates to being picked on. When they hear such references, ask them to call out, "Stop!" Then resume reading until you come to another reference.

2. Connect the Bible passage to today's story. Say: *The Bible passage is part of Jesus' famous Sermon on the Mount. In verses 10-12, Jesus warned his listeners that they wouldn't always be popular with others because of their association with him. In fact, they would be tortured and persecuted for believing in him. Notice that this persecution could be physical or verbal. Both kinds of persecution hurt, don't they? Now here's the unusual part. Jesus said that if we are persecuted for believing in him, we will be blessed. BLESSED! How does Jesus say we will be blessed?* Discuss briefly what they heard in the Bible reading about what it means to be blessed by persecution.

Transition comment: *Persecution, imprisonment, and martyrdom have often been part of the story of God's people through the centuries. Today we are going to find out what it meant for the Anabaptist friends we have been following.*

3. Perform the skit "Standing Up to Death."

4. Storytelling and discussion. Hand out copies of "About Those Women." Read through the introduction, then ask them to read one or both stories in small groups. Discuss: How do these pictures of Anabaptist women compare to our ideas of the role of women 400 years ago, and how do they challenge our own ways of seeing gender today?

Option: In addition to, or instead of point 4: Read or tell one of the other stories from the book *On Fire for Christ*. The story of Dirk Willems is especially moving, but is not included elsewhere in this curriculum.

1. Ask youth to answer the following True and False statements by standing if they think it is true and remaining seated if they think it is false.

Thanks to the Anabaptists, we can choose when we want to be baptized. (TRUE, although it is a bit of a trick question. The Anabaptists would say we should be baptized only when we're able to make an adult decision to follow Christ.)

Thanks to the Anabaptist movement, we can worship and read the Bible whenever and wherever we want to today. (FALSE. It was really the larger Reformation movement that encouraged people to read and study their Bibles. The Anabaptists got in trouble, however, for interpreting the Bible in ways that didn't fit with either the Protestant or Catholic teaching.)

Christians persecute other Christians. (Sad but TRUE). Even since the early Anabaptists, some Christian groups work against other Christians who don't agree with them. You may wish to talk briefly about contemporary examples, say, in South America (Catholics and evangelicals) or Russia (Orthodox versus other groups).

The early Anabaptists died for their faith, but Christian martyrdom doesn't happen anymore in today's world. (FALSE. Christians are being martyred in some countries that have state religions.)

Jesus was an Anabaptist. (FALSE—but you could generate some discussion around this.)

2. Ask youth to imagine that it is 500 years in the future. A class of young people is studying "Anabaptists of the 21st Century," and your name is on the list! What is being said about you? What kind of Anabaptist were you? What did you do in your lifetime?

Give them several options of how to make their presentations:

• Write it down.
• Illustrate it with markers on paper.

- Write a song (put new words to a tune they already know)
- Act it out. Have a "TV News Reporter" interview the student, who is talking about himself or herself. Example: Clarke says: "Oh yes, Carla. She was interesting. You wouldn't have known in high school that she was an Anabaptist, but then she got real involved in protesting against the government's death penalty."

After a few minutes, invite youth to share what they said about themselves.

Option 2: Have someone share with the class who has been persecuted in one way or another for their beliefs. Ask them what kept them strong in those circumstances.

RESPOND

Ask youth to take the screws (Hear and Enter 3) home with them as a reminder of the pain that the Anabaptists suffered, and to remind them that God is with them when they suffer for standing up for their beliefs. Close with prayer, asking God to help us live out the beliefs that our Anabaptist ancestors were willing to die for.

REFLECT AND LOOK AHEAD
Did the youth get a small sense of what the Anabaptists endured because of their faith?

Are they thinking about their response to Jesus' invitation to them to live their lives with and for him?

If you have not done so already, prepare to show the film *The Radicals* (see next session).

If you are planning to use the congregational activity "About Those Anabaptists!" (Appendix A), be in touch with the appropriate people in leadership to put it on the calendar.

DIGGING DEEPER
Jesus, on a number of occasions, told his disciples that they would be persecuted and opposed for being his followers. In today's Scripture text Jesus even promises blessing and reward for those who are faithful to him through persecution: "Your reward is great in heaven" (Matt. 5:12). Stories of faithfulness through difficulty and opposition have multiplied throughout the history of the church, and they have inspired and sustained Christians in many settings.

The *Martyrs Mirror* has probably been the most-read

volume among Mennonites since it was published in the 17th century. It is a heavy book—heavy in the weight of story upon story, and heavy in the content of the stories themselves. And this is a heavy session for the students to hear and experience, but a very important one. It is also important for students to know that persecution and torture was not unique to the Anabaptists or to their time period. Standing up for one's faith has meant pain, suffering, and death for many Christians, both in and outside of the Anabaptist and Mennonite traditions.

As you prepare for this lesson, you may want to read the stories of others who have been willing to suffer for their faith and convictions. The *Martyrs Mirror* has many stories from the 16th century, some of which are recounted in more popular form in *On Fire for Christ. Through Fire and Water* (see introduction) also has stories of more recent Anabaptist heroes of faith. The stories of a Russian Mennonite living in Central Asia in the 1880s and a Pennsylvania Mennonite in 1918 are two good examples. (*Through Fire and Water*, pages 16-19) More recent examples from other cultures include those of Luis A. Lumibao and Naka Gininda (pages 325-328).

There are stories in your congregation. They may or may not be stories of lives being physically threatened. But if there are Christians, there are stories of what it means to follow Christ's upside-down approach to life. Tell the stories. Share them with the youth. Invite the youth to share their stories too.

HANDOUTS
Standing Up to Death
About Those Women

STANDING UP TO DEATH
SKIT

Characters

Felix Manz, the first Anabaptist martyr
George Blaurock, early Anabaptist leader
Ulrich Zwingli, reformer in Zurich, opposed to the Anabaptists
Woman, a bystander to the events

Materials

Sharp screws for each student
2 lengths of rope, long enough to tie hands and feet

FELIX: (*Walks around, shaking a bag with the screws in it.*) You wanna know how I'm doing? Here, let me show you how I'm doing. No, I can't really show you—some of you would probably faint. But let me give you a SMALL idea anyhow. (*He passes out one screw to each person.*)

Now, put that in your hand or on your thumb and twist it. (*He demonstrates.*) HARD! Go ahead! Twist it until you see some blood. You don't want to do that? It hurts?

Yeah, persecution hurts. Don't I know. Every time I get thrown in prison for preaching and baptizing adults, they torture me. With screws like this, and much worse. And I'm not the only one. All of us Anabaptists are in danger, and many have been tortured in prison. You'd think we're stupid or something, asking for this torture.

ULRICH: You *are* stupid, Felix. I don't know what's gotten into your head, but it's gonna get you killed. I hate to see that, but you're asking for it.

FELIX: So I've heard. I've heard that the government has declared the death penalty for anyone baptizing adults. And you, my friend, would sentence me to death?

ULRICH: You sentence yourself, Felix.

GEORGE: We obey God, not the government. You used to believe that, Ulrich. What happened to you?

ULRICH: What happened to me is that I began a new church—you know that. The Reformed Church. We are forbidding Catholic services in Zurich. We are replacing the Catholic church in Zurich. I thought that's what you wanted—to break away from the Catholic church.

GEORGE: We did. But you changed your mind. At one time you said the Bible doesn't support infant baptism. Now you are preaching that adult baptism is ridiculous and that anyone practicing it should be punished. What *do* you believe, Ulrich?

ULRICH: I believe that you Anabaptists are misguided and lost, and I will not allow you to continue to influence others and lead them astray too.

FELIX: You can't stop us.

ULRICH: Oh yes we can. (*He pulls out the rope and ties Felix's hands and feet together.*) There, now we're going to make a trip out to the river.

WOMAN: Felix Manz was taken to the river and was asked one more time to give up his Anabaptist faith. He refused. On January 5, 1527, he was thrown into the water and drowned. He was the first Anabaptist martyr.

GEORGE: Two years after Felix went to be with the Lord, it was my turn. I was sentenced to death by fire. As the flames began to burn my feet and legs, I wanted my friends to know that I was still holding onto my faith, still trusting God. So I pointed my fingers toward heaven. (*Demonstrate this.*)

WOMAN: It was horrible to see him burning alive. The government thought surely this would stop our movement. But instead, it had the opposite effect. Seeing our friends being strong in their faith gave us new strength. We realized that there is something much worse than death—and that is being unfaithful to God. With God, we may die, but we live on for eternity.

ABOUT THOSE *Women*

You will notice that most of the stories in *Adventures with the Anabaptists* are about men. In the 16th century, it was men who had the positions of leadership, men who did most of the writing and preaching, and men who got into the history books. At the same time, the Anabaptist movement depended on thousands of courageous women in a way that the larger Reformation did not. Many Anabaptist women spoke their faith boldly before the government. Some gave speeches that showed they had studied the Bible extensively. A few, like Helene of Freyburg, were powerful leaders. And when it came to torture and martyrdom, women were not spared. Thousands were torn away from their families and children and willingly gave their lives for Christ.

The Milkmaid Martyr

When she was a child, Elizabeth Dirks became a nun in the Catholic church of Holland. When she was 12 years old she heard stories about heretics being killed because they didn't believe everything the Catholic church taught. That made her curious. She decided to study the Bible for herself and see what all of the commotion was about. Pretty soon she doubted some of the church's teachings, too, and she talked to other nuns about her questions. The nuns weren't all thrilled about this kid asking questions, so they imprisoned her in the convent for a year on suspicion of heresy.

STOP: What do you think heresy means? (According to Meriam Webster's Collegiate Dictionary it is "adherence to a religious opinion contrary to church dogma.")

Since Elizabeth was so young, some of the nuns felt sorry for her. They helped her escape by disguising her as a milkmaid. She walked away from the convent and to the home of some Anabaptists, who took her in. She was soon baptized and became active in the Anabaptist church. She lived with a widow, and the two of them shared their faith with others.

Elizabeth was arrested and accused of heresy again and of being Menno Simons' wife. (She wasn't.) At her trial, the council ordered her to give them the names of people she'd taught and the person who baptized her. They asked her about her beliefs and gave her a bad time for leaving the Catholic church. She willingly told them about her Anabaptist beliefs but she refused to reveal anyone else's name.

STOP: From what you remember of previous sessions, what Anabaptist beliefs was Elizabeth in trouble for?

When Elizabeth refused to reveal any names and wouldn't change her beliefs, she was taken to a torture chamber. Thumbscrews were put on her thumbs and forefingers until blood squirted out of her nails. Elizabeth prayed hard. Then the executioner put screws on her shins and pulled on them until her joints were dislocated. Elizabeth screamed for God's help, but still did not say any names. At that point, they gave her the death sentence. Elizabeth Dirks was drowned for her beliefs on May 27, 1549.

Queen in the Castle

Helene of Freyburg was a woman of nobility. She married a baron, they had three sons, and together they lived in a castle near the town of Kitzbuhel in Tyrol, Austria. You might say she had "the good life."

The town of Kitzbuhel was a center for Anabaptists, and Helene came into contact with this group of people. One thing led to another, and she not only became an Anabaptist, she also shared her castle with them as a place where they could hide and worship. Here the government authorities wouldn't look for them. She even gave money to the Anabaptist cause.

Helene's good life didn't last long after she started hanging out with the Anabaptists. When someone reported that she was a baptized member, a warrant was issued for her arrest.

Rather than be arrested, Helene ran away, leaving her husband and sons behind. She traveled from town to town, but she knew she would have to get clear out of the country if she didn't want the government to catch up with her. She ended up in Constance, where she once again became involved with Anabaptists. In fact, she was so influential among the Anabaptists there that the city council forced her to leave that city! This was one powerful woman!

Meanwhile, back at home, Helene's family and friends were begging the government to let her return. They agreed, on one condition—that she would recant.

STOP. What does recant mean? (Webster's: "to withdraw or repudiate (a statement or belief) publicly.")

Helene did come back home, and she even agreed to recant. The government was thrilled to hear this, and added that she had to do it in a church filled with people. To have someone of her nobility and influence recant in front of a large group would be much better for their cause against the Anabaptists.

Helene said, "No way"— she would only do it privately. The government gave in, and Helene said she would stop her erring ways. Then she left again. This time she ended up in Augsburg, and for the next 11 years she helped lead the Anabaptists there, holding church services in her home.

No, she'd never given up her Anabaptist beliefs. And guess what happened to her. Yes, she got in trouble with the law again, and was accused of holding Anabaptist meetings in her home, which was illegal. When brought before the city council, she said they weren't big meetings—just a few people talking about the Word of God. As punishment, this noble woman was put in chains for a night and then expelled from Augsburg.

Do you get the feeling Helene was on the list of "Ten Most Unwanted Anabaptists"?

When her husband died, Helene's sons begged the city council to let her live in Augsburg again. The council agreed, and once she got there, she was right back to her old ways. One of the people she talked to was her tailor, Hans Jacob Schneider. He became an Anabaptist, and later, he was a leader in the Anabaptist church.

Helene was known as a "lay leader" among the Anabaptists, meaning that she was not in an official role of leadership. But she did a lot for the movement. Because she was from a noble family, she could relate to nobility and commoners alike. Her leadership was instrumental in the survival of the Anabaptist movement.

SESSION 6
PREPARATION

THIS WE BELIEVE

Scripture text: Ephesians 2:19-22

Key verse: You are no longer strangers and aliens, but you are citizens with the saints and also members of the household of God. (Ephesians 2:19)

Faith focus: The early Anabaptists discussed and wrote down statements that expressed the foundations of their beliefs.

Session goal: To introduce youth to Anabaptist beliefs as outlined in the Schleithem Confession, and to help them think about and express what they believe.

Materials and advance preparation needed:
Copies of the handouts "This They Believe" and "The Schleitheim Confession"
- Pencils
- Pieces of paper with the Scripture printed on them
- A basket of goodies or prizes. This could be food, such as fruit, chips, candy, or small gifts. There should be enough variety for everyone to be able to choose.

EXPLORATION

Tell youth that you will go around the group and ask them, one at a time, to say what they believe about the word you give them. They can say the first thing that comes to mind, or they can ask to pass if they need to think about it. If they pass, come back to them later and ask them for an answer. Suggested words (add to or change the list as you wish):

cars	tattoos
parents	computers
contemporary Christian music	chocolate
football	the opposite sex
your country	cats
teachers	the earth

Expect answers such as: "Football is the best sport" or "The earth is experiencing global warming."

FOCUS
(5 minutes)

CONNECT
(5 minutes)

Go back through the list and ask youth how they formed their beliefs about these things. Through personal experiences? Through what they've been told by others? Through studying the subject? Recognize that at this stage in their lives and on these "light" topics, their responses may not be very thought provoking. That's okay. Say: *Today we're going to find out what the Anabaptists believed about cars, computers, football, cats, tatoos, contemporary Christian music, the opposite sex, teachers, parents, chocolate, their country, and the earth.* When the laughter subsides, say: *Actually, the Anabaptists had some pretty definite beliefs about God and the church, and they wanted to make those beliefs public. When they did, however, they got in trouble, and had to defend those beliefs in court.*

HEAR AND ENTER
(25 minutes)

1. Bible study. Divide the class into eight groups of one or more students each. If you have less people, combine groups. For example, 2 and 3 could be combined, and 6 and 7. Give each group one of the following parts of today's Scripture, written on a slip of paper.

Group 1: So then, you are no longer strangers and aliens
Group 2: but you are citizens with the saints
Group 3: and also members of the household of God,
Group 4: built upon the foundation of the apostles and prophets
Group 5: with Christ Jesus himself as the cornerstone.
Group 6: In him the whole structure is joined together
Group 7: and grows into a holy temple in the Lord;
Group 8: in whom you also are built together spiritually into a dwelling place for God.

Explain that this text was part of a letter the apostle Paul wrote to Christians in Ephesus. Give the groups time to memorize their lines, then ask them to stand in turn to recite their parts in order. Do this several times. Then let them sit down and ask: *So, what is going on in these verses? Why do you think Paul would have written this to them?*

Then say: *Ever since the church began, people have been putting down statements about what they believe. Sometimes the church will work together on a statement of what they all believe so that they can all be on the same page. Sometimes leaders will make statements that sum up what the church believes. The passage we just read is a statement that Paul made about what the church was. The household of God, Paul said, is people. People are the church. The church is the family of God. That idea was also a very important part of what the Anabaptists believed. Let's find out what important things they believed about the Christian faith and the church.*

2. Pass out "This They Believe." Ask youth to get together in the same groups they had for the Scripture memorization. As a group, they should go through the handout and write down what they think the Anabaptists believed about each topic. Some of the topics are from the Schleitheim Confession, others are modern-day or weren't addressed by the Schleitheim Confession. Encourage the youth to think about what they know about the Anabaptists from the lessons so far, and to guess what they would have said even if they don't know for sure.

3. Pass out the "The Schleitheim Confession." Read the story of Michael Sattler together, including the summary of the Confession. At the place marked in the reading, compare what the youth said about the topics in "This They Believe" with what the Schleitheim Confession said on those topics. Discuss the other topics as well, asking youth to explain how they decided what the Anabaptists believed.

Option 1: *Have the youth take turns "confessing" what they feel about each point in the Schleitheim Confession. Emphasize that they do not have to agree. This is a time to think about it and evaluate it for themselves. Let them know that when they make their "confession," they will be rewarded rather than persecuted.* After each person has stated his or her response, let them choose something from the basket of goodies/prizes.

Option 2: Have volunteers come up and "state their case" as if they were Anabaptists facing a court on what they believe. You, or someone you appoint, could be the interrogator, introducing each point of faith using the items on "This They Believe." Give volunteers first choices of the goodies or prizes, then share the prizes around the group.

Option 3: In groups of four or five, have the youth reenact the Anabaptists' meeting at Schleitheim. Have them draft a brief confession of faith on the following points:

APPLY
(8 minutes)

What makes someone a Christian?
What does baptism mean?
What is the church, and what are the membership requirements?

Emphasize that they will obviously not be able to give their confession the same polish that the Schleitheim group did to theirs, but that they're simply getting a sense of what it felt like to summarize what beliefs the group held in common. When they are through, ask for volunteers from the groups to read their statements. Applaud after each one.

RESPOND
(2 minutes)

Eyes-open prayer: Let the youth know you are going to pray with your eyes open. In your prayer, thank God for each person by name and ask God to be with each one as they make decisions on what they believe. Personalize it as much as you want to, based on what you heard them sharing in the session.

REFLECT AND LOOK AHEAD
Did the youth understand the beliefs stated in the Schleitheim Confession? Did they make the connection between what happened hundreds of years ago and the beliefs of Anabaptist churches today?

Pick a night for the class to come to your home, or use an extra class session or two to watch *The Radicals* (produced by Gateway Films/Vision Video). Caution: there is some violence in this film—you will want to preview it and perhaps let parents know about the violence. This film portrays the young Anabaptists in Switzerland, particularly Michael Sattler, and brings martyrdom into stark reality. Whether you do it in one or several sessions, you are strongly encouraged to watch this film with your class. You should be able to check it out through your church library or resource center, or buy it through Mennonite Publishing House (1 800 743-2484), Mennonite Media (1 800 999-3534), or a local Provident or other bookstore.

DIGGING DEEPER
Within two years after George Blaurock performed the first believer's baptism of the Anabaptist movement, it was clear that the government authorities would not allow Anabaptism to spread and become dominant. Luther and Zwingli were establishing territorial state churches, but when some Anabaptist leaders attempted to begin their own fellowships, the powers

that be seemed to win out. One example was Waldshut, a town of about 7,000 in southern Germany. Hundreds of people were baptized in this town, and Anabaptism became the dominant faith. But when Austrian forces attacked the town and the Anabaptist leader, Balthasar Hubmaier, had to flee, the old Catholic faith was reintroduced.

The Anabaptists realized that they would be rejected and persecuted as believers, and that people would hate their church. They also believed that small Christian communities were to let their light shine in a dark world, and that individual believers gathered in congregations were to model for the world what it meant to be disciples of Jesus.

This vision of a separated Christian community was first drafted in 1527 in a document called "Brotherly Union," better known as the Schleitheim Confession. A group of Anabaptists had gathered for a secret meeting in Schleitheim, a small town in northern Switzerland, to discuss and debate issues regarding the Christian faith and church. In the end, they agreed to accept a document drafted by Michael Sattler that contained seven articles as their guidelines. (See handout. Also, the complete text of the Schleitheim Confession can be found at several websites, including that of the Mennonite Historical Society of Canada, which has an online encyclopedia about Mennonites http://www.mhsc.ca.)

Michael Sattler had been a monk before he left the Catholic church and joined the Anabaptists. His life in the monastery influenced the writing of the Schleitheim articles. Anabaptist ideals such as separation from the world and the role of the Christian community as a model of Jesus' way had roots in Benedictine monasticism.

Not all Anabaptists accepted the Schleitheim articles. Balthasar Hubmaier argued that there were times when Christians must use the sword in defense of their government or country. Later, Menno Simons did not draw the line between the kingdom of God and the kingdom of the world as sharply as the Swiss Brethren did. Nevertheless, the Schleitheim Confession became the basis for all subsequent Mennonite confessions of faith.

HANDOUTS
This They Believe
The Schleitheim Confession

This they Believe

Write down what you think the Anabaptists believed about:

1. Baptism

2. Excommunication (expelling a person from the church for abandoning his or her Christian life)

3. The Lord's Supper (Communion) (Who takes it? Is it the body and blood of Jesus?)

4. Interaction with the world

5. Pastors
Who is qualified?

What kind of people should they be?

What is their job?

6. Violence towards others
Towards bad people in general

Towards people who are hurting them

7. Involvement with the government
Running for public office

8. Swearing an oath in court or when taking a public office

9. Serving in the military

10. Divorce

11. The use of a church's budget money
What should be the priorities?

12. Owning a handgun for self-protection

13. Going to a movie rated R

14. Telling other people about your faith

The Schleitheim Confession

Conrad Grebel was dead. Felix Manz was dead. With some of the first Anabaptist leaders gone, who would lead the people? The government was after them, and they had no one to inspire and lead them. Some believers, fearing persecution, kept very quiet about their beliefs. Others weren't even sure what they believed.

Enter Michael Sattler. Born in Germany, he led a comfortable life—first as a monk, then as a prior, a leader in the monastery. His was an important position in the church, and from his "inside perspective" he saw the corruption. He saw pastors being greedy and wanting power. He saw drinking and loose morals among the monks and priests, and it upset him.

After studying the Bible, Michael knew what he had to do; he had to leave the Catholic church. He also knew that if he left, he would lose his income and he would be persecuted. But he left the monastery, married Margaretha, who left her position as a nun, and went to live with the Anabaptists near Zurich, Switzerland.

Michael and Margaretha soon rose to roles of leadership among the struggling Anabaptists. At that time differing and conflicting ideas were tearing the Anabaptists apart, and the movement could have died if someone didn't do something. On February 24, 1527, Michael and Margaretha and several other leaders (probably including George Blaurock) met secretly in the town of Schleitheim, Switzerland. They discussed the confusion among the Anabaptists, and came up with a list of statements of what Anabaptists believed. These statements came to be known as "The Schleitheim Confession." The main points were as follows:

1. **Baptism** is for those who repent and want to follow Jesus.
2. **Excommunication** is for those who fall away from their Christian life. First the person is talked to in private, then if necessary he or she is brought in front of the congregation. If the person doesn't change, then he or she is expelled from the church. (See Matt. 18.)
3. **The Lord's Supper** is for those who have been baptized and through baptism are part of God's congregation.
4. **Separation from the world** means to be separated from the evil and sin of the world.

5. **Pastors** in the church shall be [persons] of good reputation. They are to take care of the church by teaching, counseling, and helping others to lead Christian lives.

6. **The use of the "sword"** is for the worldly government to punish evil people and to protect the good people. Therefore, Christians should never resort to violence, even for self-protection.

7. **Swearing an oath** is against what Jesus taught. Christians should answer with a simple yes or no.

(Pause here and compare this list to the "This They Believe" handout that you worked on.)

Three months after The Schleitheim Confession was drafted, Michael, Margaretha, and other Anabaptists were arrested. Nine charges were brought against Sattler, including:
—Sattler taught that the body and blood of Jesus are not really present in the bread and wine of communion.
—Sattler taught that infant baptism does not guarantee a person's salvation.
—Sattler said that people should not swear an oath before court authorities.
—Sattler served the bread and wine on a plate for the Lord's Supper.
—Sattler abandoned his commitments as a monk, and he got married.

Sattler defended himself and said he wasn't out to overthrow the church. When he explained his faith to the judges, they just laughed at him. The more he talked, the angrier they became. The called him an "arch heretic," an accusation that called for him to die.

Michael Sattler was so popular among the people that a guard was posted to watch him constantly so the people wouldn't rebel against the authorities and break him out of jail. On May 21, 1527, in Rottenburg, Germany, Sattler's tongue was cut out, he was burned with hot tongs, then tied to a ladder. A bag of gunpowder was tied around his neck, and he was set on fire. His last words were "Father, I commend my spirit into your hands." Ten days later, his wife Margaretha was drowned for her faith.

SESSION 7
PREPARATION

PROMISES, PROMISES

Scripture texts: Genesis 9:8-17; Luke 22:14-20

Key verse: I have set my rainbow in the clouds, and it shall be a sign of the covenant between me and the earth. (Genesis 9:13)

Faith focus: God makes promises of salvation and forgiveness, and keeps them faithfully.

Session goal: To introduce the youth to Menno Simons and to make them aware of the Anabaptist belief about the "new covenant" as symbolized in the Lord's Supper.

Materials and advance preparation needed:
- An assortment of symbols. Examples: item with the Nike swoosh on it; a flag from a country, state or province; a business logo; item with a school mascot; a church logo; a picture of the Statue of Liberty or the Parliament buildings, etc.
- Two copies of the skit "Menno Who?" and two students (boy and girl) prepared to perform it. It is important to rehearse the skit several times ahead of time.
- A loaf of French bread and a pitcher of grape juice
- Small paper cups
- Pipe cleaners or big colorful paper clips

EXPLORATION

If you have enough symbols for each youth, hand them out. If not, hold them up one by one, then discuss each in turn. Ask youth to say what each symbol represents? What are some of the larger meanings behind it? (The Nike swoosh doesn't just mean the Nike company. Does it mean "the best"? Does it mean people in sweat shops making shoes?) Ask youth about other symbols they can think of, and what they mean.

FOCUS
(5 minutes)

Ask youth to name symbols they have run across in the Bible, or in the church, and talk about what they mean. Be prepared to suggest anointing (e.g., David) baptism, communion.

CONNECT
(5 minutes)

Then say: *Today we're going to talk about two symbols we read about in the Bible, and we're going to meet a guy named Menno Simons. Does anyone know who Menno Simons is?* After that question is answered, ask: *Does anyone know what Menno Simons and symbols have to do with each other?* (If not, don't answer it at this point.)

HEAR AND ENTER
(20 minutes)

1. Storytelling. Ask youth to tell the story of Noah and the flood. Encourage them with questions such as: *Who was involved? What happened? What was the outcome?* When you feel confident that they recalled the whole story, ask one of them to read Genesis 9:8-17. Ask: *Is there something SYMBOLIC going on here? What? What does God say in connection with the rainbow? What is a covenant?* God makes a covenant—a promise—that the earth will never again experience a total flood. God also says that the rainbow will be a reminder of that promise.

Say: *Then, just a few years after the flood, Menno showed up on the scene. (Pause for reactions.) Okay, I was just checking to see if you were still awake and paying attention.*

Actually, it was quite a while later—thousands of years—that Menno Simons became a part of our story. He struggled with another symbol of God's promise that was very important to both the Anabaptists and the rulers in the state churches in the 1500s. Let's hear it out.

2. Skit: "Menno Who?" Before your actors perform, introduce the skit by saying that the characters, Menno and Ursula, were real, but the particular event is fictional. The skit illustrates true issues that Menno and Ursula faced in their lives.

3. Brief discussion. Leave a few moments for youth to ask questions or comment on the story. You may wish to note that there were plenty of youth who were arrested for being Anabaptists. Society did not include a separate "youth" subculture and the state did not have a special category for juvenile crime.

APPLY
(5 minutes)

Pass around the loaf of bread and ask each youth to take a piece off and eat it as it goes by. Then pass out small cups of grape juice and tell them to drink it. When that's done, ask, *"What did we just do?"* If they say "We took communion," explain that no, they didn't. If they say "We had some bread and juice," affirm them in their observation.

Explain: *Celebrating the Lord's Supper happens for us*

with bread and grape juice, that is true. But it happens in a setting where believers gather together to remember God's promise that through Jesus God brings us new life and forgiveness from our sin. Usually, communion is led by a recognized spiritual leader, such as a pastor. Celebrating the Lord's Supper is a special occasion—special because of the way the meal symbolizes God's commitment to us and our own commitment to follow Jesus as our Lord, as part of the family of faith.. Just as the rainbow symbolized God's promise to humanity, this meal symbolizes what Jesus did for us by living and dying for us. You've probably heard the story before, but let's listen to that first story of communion. (At this point have a student read the story of the Last Supper from Luke 22:14-20.)

One of the main disagreements between Menno Simons and the Catholic church was over the meaning of the Lord's Supper. The church taught that the bread and wine literally became the body and blood of Jesus. It was treated almost as a medicine to take away sins. From his study of the Bible, however, Menno preached that it was a meal that symbolized God's covenant with us in Christ. We may not believe that the bread and juice really become the body and blood of Jesus like the Catholics do, but we do believe communion is a sacred, symbolic event. What we did here was to eat some bread and drink some juice. When a person is ready to promise to follow Jesus and become a part of the church family, then that person is ready to take communion.

Hand out pipe cleaners or big colorful paper clips. Ask youth to make a symbol of what they feel is God's most important promise to them. As a closing sharing and prayer time, go around the group and have each person hold up his or her symbol and say "Thank you, God, for your promise of…

REFLECT AND LOOK AHEAD

Did the youth understand the importance of symbols in our spiritual lives? Did they become better acquainted with the early Anabaptists, especially Menno Simons? Did they see the distinction between what the Catholic church believed about the Lord's Supper and what Mennonites believe?

DIGGING DEEPER

As you learned in the skit "Menno Who?" Menno Simons began to have questions about several aspects of the Catholic church, but he didn't leave the priesthood. His job was just too cushy. When a group of

RESPOND
(5 minutes)

Draw on paper

fanatical Anabaptists began acting violently, however, Menno finally came to terms with what he believed and how he was living.

The Anabaptists of Muenster, in Germany, were forcing people to be baptized and even killed anyone who didn't agree with them. As a result, they were crushed by the state authorities, and were killed themselves. This was not the kind of Anabaptism Menno had secretly come to admire. He wrote: "The blood of these people...fell so hot upon my heart that I could not stand it, nor find rest in my soul.... I saw that these zealous children, although in error, willingly gave their lives...for their doctrine and their faith. And I was one...who had disclosed to some of them the abominations of the papal system. But I...continued in my comfortable life...simply in order that I might enjoy physical comfort and escape the Cross of Christ."

Menno knew what he had to do. Tearfully he asked God for forgiveness, to create within him a clean heart and to bestow upon him "wisdom, spirit, and courage" for a new life in Christ. In January 1536, Menno renounced all "worldly reputation, name, and fame." He submitted to stress and poverty, and left his home community and parish to start an "underground" existence. Among the lowly and persecuted believers, Menno found a new spiritual home and his most important life's work. (For the fascinating story of Menno's conversion and leadership, see chapter 5 of *Through Fire and Water.*)

A powerful point to make with your youth in this lesson is that the founder of the Mennonite church was far from perfect himself. He lived a lie for many years because it was more comfortable. But God promises never to give up on us, and Menno finally not only "saw the light" but decided to live it as well. Then, with the wisdom, spirit, and courage that he asked for and that God gave him, Menno went on to become the much needed leader of the struggling Anabaptists.

HANDOUT
Menno Who?

Menno WHO?

(a two-person drama)

Characters: Menno Simons
                Ursula Hellrigel

Ursula is seated. Menno is standing, knocking on an imaginary door that separates them from each other.

MENNO: *(knocking with his hand)* Knock knock!

URSULA: Who's there?

MENNO: Menno!

URSULA: Menno who?

MENNO: Menno Night.

URSULA: I don't know any Menno Nights.

MENNO: Look, could you open the door? I'm afraid the authorities are after me and I need a place to hide for a little while.

Ursula stands up and opens the door. Menno comes in and closes the door behind him. Ursula looks him over.

URSULA: You look like Menno Simons, not Menno Night.

MENNO: I am Menno Simons, knocking on your door at night. Look, it was a bad joke. Thanks for letting me in.

URSULA: No problem. I'm glad to be of assistance. Sit down, please.*(Menno sits down.)*

MENNO: Thanks. I have been walking for quite awhile. This business of being an Anabaptist is hard on the body, mind, and soul.

URSULA: I know what you mean.

MENNO: I'd heard that this family might give me shelter, but I don't know anything about you. Have the authorities been after you too?

URSULA: That's a long story.

MENNO: Tell me! I have time—if you do.

URSULA: Well, I grew up in Switzerland, and I got involved with the Anabaptists when I was a teenager.

MENNO: Wasn't that scary?

URSULA: Sure. I was afraid of the authorities finding out about my beliefs and putting me in prison. Then one day it happened. They put me in jail. Oh, that was a horrible place.

MENNO: How old were you?

URSULA: Seventeen.

MENNO: Amazing. I can't imagine going to jail as a teenager for something you believe.

URSULA: Really? But you are the well-known Menno Simons. Weren't you a devout person as a teenager?

MENNO: Devout? Maybe—in a different way. I was born in Holland. My parents were farmers, and strict Catholics. They brought me up to serve and worship God. I studied to be a priest, and I became a priest when I was 28.

URSULA: Then surely you were a devout believer.

MENNO: Oh, I knew the things to say and do. I performed mass and baptized babies and all the things that priests do. But in my free time, I tipped the bottle quite a bit, and played my share of cards too.

URSULA: I had no idea.

MENNO: I take it you didn't do any of that as a teenager?

URSULA: Even if I'd wanted to, they didn't serve drinks or offer playing cards to prisoners.

MENNO: How long were you in jail?

URSULA: Five years.

MENNO: Five years!?!?!!

URSULA: Five very long years, from when I was 17 until 22.

MENNO: How did they treat you?

URSULA: At the beginning, they brought in a preacher to try to convince us to change our minds. I think they didn't really want to keep us there, and hoped we would recant and then they could release us. But when we didn't recant, they did other things to try to get me to change my mind.

MENNO: Were you tortured?

URSULA: Not like some of the adults. They put me on a very meager diet, and limited my clothing. I was always hungry, and so cold. Five years of that...it was awful. One time they tied me to the feet of another prisoner who was tortured and racked. I can't describe how horrible that was.

MENNO: I can't imagine. It makes me feel like such a coward.

URSULA: Why?

MENNO: Because there came a time when I began to question things about the beliefs of the church. Like whether or not the bread and wine really become the body of Jesus. I started to read the Bible—something I'd done very little of up to that point. And from what I read, I realized that the bread and wine are symbols of Christ's body and blood—reminders of God's love for us, not a magic substance that wipes out our sins. The meal is a time of communion with God and fellowship with other committed believers, not just a ritual that a priest performs for us.

URSULA: You were a priest when you began to realize this?

MENNO: Yes. And not only that. I began to hear about people who were being persecuted and killed because they believed the Bible taught things about communion and baptism that were different from what the state church taught. These were the Anabaptists, who believed that people should be baptized only when they're old enough to understand. I'd never questioned infant baptism, so I began to look at the Bible for answers on that too. I couldn't find anything that supported infant baptism. That meant I had two big areas where I'd come to conclusions opposite from those of the Catholic church.

URSULA: So you left the priesthood.

MENNO: Nope, I just kept my thoughts to myself. In fact, I got promoted. I kept on practicing one thing and believing another. That's why I think it is so amazing that even though you were young, you were willing to go to jail and suffer for your beliefs. I didn't have the guts to do that for years. How did you finally get out of prison?

URSULA: They decided to release me if I promised not to return to my home town. I did agree to leave, but I refused to swear that I'd never return. They let me go anyway—thanks be to God!! I moved to this Anabaptist community, and here I am.

MENNO: I am so thankful that you are here. God has certainly been with you. It is people like you who continue to encourage me.

URSULA: You still haven't told me how you went from being a priest to a leader of the Anabaptists.

MENNO: That is another long story. . . .

SESSION 8
PREPARATION

PEACE IT TOGETHER

Scripture text: Matthew 5:38-48

Key verse: Love your enemies and pray for those who persecute you. (Matthew 5:44)

Faith focus: Menno Simons broke away from the Catholic church and joined the Anabaptists after seeing a group of Anabaptists using violence to acheive their purposes.

Session goal: To help youth see that the Anabaptists certainly were not "perfect," and that the roots of the peace position were challenged but became stronger as a result.

Materials and advance preparation needed:
- Someone to come into the class with a picnic basket and "force" students to eat a snack
- Snack food
- Handout: "Believe It or Not"
- Handout: "Menno, MCC, Mildred, and Me" (Note: "MCC" in this handout refers to Mennonite Central Committee, the Mennonite agency that does relief, development, and peace promotion around the world. If your group is not Mennonite, you may wish to adapt this handout to focus on another organization that works for peace.)

EXPLORATION

Ask youth to close their hands into a fist. Ask: *What can you do with your closed hands?* Have them demonstrate it, if you wish. Then ask them to open their hands, palms up. Ask: *What can you do with open hands?* Demonstrate it.

FOCUS
(5 minutes)

Read the following list of people, one at a time. Ask youth to say whether that person would be a "closed-fist" person or an "open-hand" person:

CONNECT
(5 minutes)

Martin Luther King	Jesus
Hitler	Saul, who became Paul
A police officer	The U.S. president/Canadian
A pastor	prime minster
Gandhi	A woman named Mildred
King David	Norman
An Anabaptist	A parent

Discuss their responses. Talk about how they decided what kind of a person each one was, and the relationship of a closed fist to what is often violent actions, and an open hand to peace-promoting actions. (Obviously these are generalizations, but they'll get the point.) Note that some of the people may be both "open hand" and "closed fist," such as police officers and Saul/Paul. The youth probably won't know who Mildred Norman is. She is known as the Peace Pilgrim and the youth will learn about her later in the lesson.

HEAR AND ENTER
(20 minutes)

1. Bible study. Ask youth to close their eyes as you read Matthew 5:38-48, one verse at a time. During a pause after each verse, they are to think about the verse and either close their hand into a fist, or open it up, depending on what the verse says.

After you have finished reading, ask them if their hands were mostly open or closed. With the exception of verse 38 and the second half of 43, their hands should be open all the time. Say: *It's natural for us as humans to be mean to people who are mean to us. It's natural for us to want to get revenge. We all know that, and we've all done it. But Jesus calls us to love people, even those who treat us badly. That's a very, very difficult thing to do.*

We've seen in our past lessons that the Anabaptists were able to follow Jesus' words. Even when they were tortured and killed, they didn't react violently to their persecutors. They almost seemed too good to be true, didn't they? Today we're going to find out that not all Anabaptists were peaceful people. Some of them used force and violence against people who didn't agree with them. But other Anabaptists strongly disagreed with that approach. Today, churches that date back to the Anabaptists are known as "peace churches."

2. Tell the following story:
Menno Simons, if you remember from the last lesson, was a Catholic priest who found he disagreed with his church on the issues of the Lord's Supper and infant

baptism. Despite the fact that he disagreed with the Catholic church, he didn't leave right away. He continued to practice as a priest while believing something different in his heart.

In 1534, in the neighboring town of Muenster, a group of Anabaptists got so fanatical about their beliefs that they forced people to be baptized as adults. Two men came to Muenster—Jan Matthys and Jan van Leyden. Calling themselves prophets, they and their followers took over the town of Muenster. Matthys taught that Muenster would be the New Jerusalem and they should prepare for the second coming of Jesus by using force. All nonbelievers would be killed, which meant that everyone in Muenster was forced to be baptized and join Matthys' group. (Does any of this sound familiar?)

The government fought back, surrounded the town and tried to get control of it again. Jan Matthys, thinking he had divine protection and wouldn't be hurt, led some of his followers out of the city to fight. They were all killed, including Jan Matthys, which meant that Jan van Leyden was now the ruler. This man was power hungry, and even called himself King David. He had 17 wives and made everybody obey his rules OR ELSE! He didn't care about the people, and soon they were starving and sick.

[*At this point, have your "guest" come storming into the room, carrying a picnic basket. The guest should quickly take over, telling students to follow her or him to another part of the room for some snacks. She or he should be very forceful verbally, and even use some light pushing if necessary. Students should be made to eat the food quickly, whether they like it or not. (Respect dietary restrictions, of course.) When they are done eating, the guest should leave as quickly as she or he arrived. Gather the students back together. Ask them what that was all about. Listen to their comments but don't make any suggestions. Then continue with the story.*]

On June 25, 1535, the army entered Muenster. The town people fought back, but many were killed. Jan van Leyden was captured and eventually put to death.

That same year another group of Anabaptists, including Peter Simons—who may have been Menno's brother—took over a monastery in Holland. Even though Menno pleaded with them to stop their violent ways, they didn't listen. When an army came and surrounded the monastery, many of the Anabaptists died, including Peter Simons.

Menno was devastated. He admired the Anabaptists

for standing up for their beliefs, but not the violence they used to achieve their purposes. It made him think about his own life. What was he doing? He was practicing one thing while believing another.

Menno decided it was time to join the Anabaptists, despite the bad reputation that the Muenster incident had given them. The government was now feeling they really had good reason to get rid of the annoying Anabaptists, even though it was only a small percentage that had been violent. Menno tried to tell the government that the Anabaptists really did believe in peace, but it was a hard sell. Menno became determined to promote the Anabaptist faith and its original beliefs. He went on to become a recognized leader of the Anabaptist movement in northern Europe.

Ask the youth if they have any more ideas about why they were forcibly told to eat a snack. If they don't catch on, explain: *This was a demonstration of something good done wrong. Just as the Anabaptist beliefs were good, the idea of a snack was good. But just as forcing people to believe was wrong, so was a snack that they were forced to participate in. It would have been so much better if they would have been invited to participate in the snack, wouldn't it? Isn't it the same with sharing the good news of Jesus? We want to invite people to follow Jesus, not scare them into it.*

3. Discussion. Distribute the handout, "Believe It or Not." Ask youth to read it and then discuss. Do they think this was coincidence? God's timing? Some of both? Do they have stories of God's timing in their lives?

APPLY
(10 minutes)

Hand out "Menno, MCC, Mildred, and Me." Go through each section with the youth, giving them time to answer the questions on the MCC and the Me sections before discussing them. On the Mennonite Central Committee questionnaire, we're assuming you are Mennonite and familiar with the organization. (If not, you may want to adapt this to your own aid or peace organization, or find MCC on the Web at http://www.mennonitecc.ca/. Answers you may need help with are: 2 (all are correct); 3 (broadly speaking, all answers are correct, since anyone can give money or put school kits together; however, staff and workers are expected to be committed Christians); and 4 (the Canadian government matches donated funds for some relief and development projects).

Option: In addition, or as an alternative to the "Mildred" story, you may wish to tell the story of Dirk Willems, who rescued his enemy, a government official pursuing him, after he fell through the ice of a frozen river. The story is used in *On Fire for Christ* (see bibliography).

RESPOND
(5 minutes)

Ask youth to close their eyes. Lead them in this meditation: *Think about yourself. Think about who you are and how you relate to important people in your life. As you think about that, allow your hands to represent how you act and feel towards them. Your hands may be in a fist, or open, or some of both. As I say some of the people that you relate to, let your hands express how you feel toward them: Parents (Pause) Close friends (Pause) Kids at school who are different from you (Pause) Your brothers and sisters (Pause) Teachers (Pause) An adult whom you really like (Pause) God (Pause) Now, open your hands with your palms up as I pray:*

God, it is not easy to be a peacemaker. Jesus did not promise it would be easy. But we know that is what you call us to be in this world—within our families, our schools, our communities, and our world. Be with us, just as you have been with so many people who follow you through the years. Amen.

REFLECT AND LOOK AHEAD

Did the youth get a good glimpse at why Mennonites believe in being peacemakers and pacifists? Are they finding ways to apply those principles in their own lives? Were they challenged to look for ways to relate peacefully to others?

If you are planning to use the congregational activity "About Those Anabaptists!" (Appendix A), make sure the time and place are clear, and begin to approach people for helping to lead it.

DIGGING DEEPER

Isn't it ironic that it took a group of violent Anabaptists to bring Menno Simons into the fold? Or, as *Through Fire and Water* states, "God must have a great sense of humor."

Certainly the events leading up to Menno Simons joining the Anabaptist movement are not particularly "holy" or inspiring. First, you have Menno discovering what he believes to be truth from the Bible, but deciding not to live it out. Second, you have a group of

Anabaptists who lived in Muenster and who, under the leadership of two self-styled prophets, Jan Matthys and Jan Van Leyden, exchanged their peaceful life and ethical standards for violence and sexual immorality. Third, as a result of the Muenster episode, the society became even more angry at the Anabaptists, and more resolved to kill them and wipe out the movement.

Enter the man who's hiding from his convictions. Menno Simons steps out of his comfortable life and into the life of a man trying to convince the government not to judge all Anabaptists by the acts of the Muenster group. He embraces the Anabaptist faith at a most crucial time and helps bring it back to its earlier intentions and beliefs.

Menno's attempts to educate the government on the difference between the violent and the peaceful Anabaptists is not so far removed from some of the challenges in the church today. The church can be tempted to use other than peaceful means to achieve its goals. Sometime, even in sharing the gospel, it is tempting to manipulate others into being Christians, or violating cultures and traditions, instead of lovingly inviting people to faith.

The early Anabaptists, Menno Simons, you, the youth in your class—we all make decisions every day that reflect how willing we are to follow the Prince of Peace in our words, thoughts, and actions.

HANDOUTS
Believe It or Not
Menno, MCC, Mildred, and Me

BELIEVE IT or NOT

For 11 years, Menno studied the Bible, questioned the Catholic beliefs, but didn't leave the church. During those 11 years, he certainly grew stronger in his faith and in his convictions.

In 1524, Menno Simons became a priest in Holland. In 1525, he started to have some doubts about the Roman Catholic church.

In 1525, in Switzerland, Conrad Grebel and his followers were baptized and began establishing the Anabaptist church and the Anabaptist movement.

In 1534, fanatical and violent Anabaptists began to take over the town of Muenster, in what is now Germany. They forced many to be baptized.

In 1535, the army took the town of Muenster back, imprisoning and killing many of the Anabaptists. That year, upset with the turn of events in Muenster, Menno decided to leave the Catholic church. He made his move just in time to save the floundering Anabaptist movement and point it in a direction that took seriously Jesus' teaching on peace, and love for enemies.

At the same time, the Anabaptist movement was growing in Switzerland and other countries. But, as we saw from our lesson today, there were also bad things happening within the movement.

What do you think? Was this:
a) luck
b) coincidence
c) God's timing
d) all of the above

1500
1550
1600

Menno, MCC, Mildred, and Me

Menno Chooses Peace

Menno Simons had an easy life. No worries.
He gave up leisure to become a hunted man.
Menno had job security. All the money he needed.
He gave it up to become poor.
Menno had a nice place to live. All the comforts he could want.
He gave it up for a life underground, running from the authorities.
Menno had it all, except peace of mind.
His heart and his convictions told him to follow Jesus and the way of peace.

MCC Promotes Peace (answers on page 70)

How much do you know about MCC? Circle the right answer(s).

1. What does MCC stand for?
   a) Mennonite Conservative Church
   b) Men, Children, and Critters
   c) Mennonite Central Committee
   d) Mennonite Congregations Committee

2. What does MCC do?
   a) Help clear former war zones of land mines
   b) Promote peace through mediation and education
   c) Provide food to starving people
   d) Help people grow their own food
   e) Help people after a disaster

3. Who works with MCC?
   a) Christians
   b) Mennonites
   c) Anabaptists
   d) Anybody who wants to

4. How does MCC get its money to do its work?
   a) the government
   b) taxes
   c) people in churches
   d) big auctions called MCC sales

5) What happens at an MCC sale?

6) Do you know someone who works for MCC? What do they do?

MILDRED NORMAN—"PEACE PILGRIM"

What would you do to promote peace?

Here's what one woman named Mildred Norman did: After praying that God would use her in service to others, she felt God calling her to walk across the United States to talk to people and to witness for peace. Mildred got rid of all of her possessions, quit eating sugar and meat, and drank only water. She became totally focused on God and her mission: to walk for peace.

On January 1, 1953, she changed her name to Peace Pilgrim. She began her walk that day at the Tournament of Roses parade in California. She wore a navy blue long-sleeved shirt and pants, and inexpensive shoes which she bought one size too big because she wanted to wiggle her toes. She wore a navy blue tunic over her shirt with pockets around the bottom, and in those pockets she carried her only possessions: a comb, toothbrush, copies of her message, letters, a pen and a map. On the front of her tunic were the words "Peace Pilgrim." On the back, it said "25,000 Miles on Foot for Peace."

Peace wore the same outfit all the time. When her clothes got dirty, she washed them in a stream where she also bathed herself. She put the clothes on wet, and the sun and wind dried them.

Peace Pilgrim walked from California to New York, never accepting a ride. She spoke her message to anyone who asked, saying "This is the way of peace—overcome evil with good, falsehood with truth, and hatred with love."

She never asked for anything. If she wasn't offered a meal, she went without. If she wasn't offered a bed for the night, she slept in the ditch, in a field, or wherever she could find. Once she slept on the seat of a fire engine!

Peace Pilgrim totally trusted God to take care of her. To her, peace meant having positive thoughts and actions and to love everyone.

For more on Mildred Norman, read Peace Pilgrim, *by Friends of Peace Pilgrim (Ocean Tree, 1982).*

ME

You've read about Menno, MCC, and Mildred. But what about you?

Name one place where you could help create peace._____

Name one person with whom you need to make peace. _____

Name one thing you are willing to do to help promote peace._____

SESSION 9
PREPERATION

A SERVANT LEADER

Scripture text: Matthew 20:20-28

Key verse: Whoever wishes to be great among you must be your servant, and whoever wishes to be first among you must be your slave. (Matthew 20:26b-27)

Faith focus: Menno Simons was a good example of what it means to be a leader with the heart and attitude of a servant.

Session goal: Help youth understand that God calls leaders who are also willing to be servants of the people they lead.

Materials and advance preparation needed:
- Pictures of people from a magazine or newspaper. They should include people of different cultures, ethnic groups, some with physical challenges, some who look "strong" and some who look "weak." Some should look like leaders according to their pose or because they have recognizable faces. Others may not look like leaders. Number the pictures. (Focus, Option 1)
- Paper and pencils for each member
- Chalkboard and chalk, or newsprint and marker
- A pair of crutches. These should be somewhere in the room, where youth can see them, but not as a focus point.
- At least five Bibles for the Scripture reading, preferably the same translation
- Copies of the drama, "Menno, This Is Your Life," for everyone in the class
- One washcloth for each class member and water

EXPLORATION

Option 1: Post the magazine and newpaper pictures on the walls around the class. Give each student paper and pencil and ask them to go around and write down on their paper the number of the picture and whether or not they think this person is a leader.

Option 2: Ask youth to name people whom they consider leaders. Make a list on the chalkboard or newsprint.

FOCUS
(5 minutes)

CONNECT (5 minutes)	Whether you used the pictures or made a list of names, ask the youth what determines who is a leader. What do they do? How do they do it? Do they have a certain appearance? Are they from a certain ethnic group? Social standing? Financial standing? Are they male or female? Young or old? What defines a leader? List the characteristics of a leader on the chalkboard or newsprint.
HEAR AND ENTER (20 minutes)	**1. Dramatic Bible reading.** Assign youth to read the following parts of the Scripture passage in Matthew 20:20-28: the mother of the sons of Zebedee; Jesus; the two sons; and a narrator. The narrator will read everything that isn't in quotes. **2. Talk about the passage.** What is it saying about leaders? Transition comment: *In our last session we learned that Menno Simons decided to join the Anabaptist group of believers because he admired their beliefs and agreed with them, even though he was a Catholic priest. Today we're going to jump way ahead in Menno's life. We're going to imagine that we are at his 65th birthday party!* **3. Perform the drama:** "Menno, This Is Your Life!" **4. Discuss:** What did they find out about Menno? Where did he live? Where did he travel? What did he do? What kind of person did he seem to be? What was his personality? His physical characteristics? As appropriate, share some of what you have learned about Menno from the Digging Deeper section below. You may wish to note that although the Anabaptists that Menno led were originally called Mennists, that name was changed later to Mennonites.
APPLY (5 minutes)	Ask the youth to compare what they learned about Menno Simons to the list of leaders you made earlier or the characteristics of a leader. What are the similarities? What are the differences? How do Menno and the other leaders match what Jesus said about a leader?
RESPOND (10 minutes)	**O**ption 1: Divide the class in half, and give wet washcloths to half of the class. Have each wash the hands of another class member. Then reverse roles, handing out fresh washcloths. Talk about the activity after it's done. How did it feel to do that? What does

this kind of activity say about leadership and service?

Explain that something similar, footwashing, was common among many of the early Anabaptists and still is practiced in many Mennonite churches today, as a sign of servanthood within the family of the church. It is based on the story of Jesus washing his disciples' feet in John 13:3-11.

Alternative: If you are feeling more adventurous, have more time available, and are sure that it is okay with the leaders of your congregation (you may wish to have them involved), conduct a footwashing ceremony with basins and towels.

Option **2:** Ask students to write the name of one person to whom they can be a servant in the next week, as well as an action plan for what they will do for or with that person. Examples: read to a younger sibling, help parents with household chores, spend time with someone in a nursing home.

With Options 1 and 2, conclude the class by saying that Jesus calls all of us, even leaders, to be servants to each other. Close with a prayer.

REFLECT AND LOOK AHEAD

Did the youth think about what makes a good leader? Did they understand that Jesus calls leaders to be servants of the people? Did they think about how physical appearance affects our perception of a leader, but Jesus calls people to be leaders based on their heart and ability to humbly serve others?

For the next session, plan how you will make the building blocks for the Apply activity. If you use the cardboard box option, you may wish to take a moment in this session to ask students to bring boxes next time.

If you are planning to use the congregational activity "About Those Anabaptists" (Appendix A), make sure the arrangements are made, and that key participants are approached.

DIGGING DEEPER

Menno Simons worked hard and traveled extensively in northern Europe—preaching, organizing churches, and giving much-needed leadership to the Anabaptists. His efforts began to pay off as rulers began to identify the differences between the violent Anabaptists and the peaceful followers of Menno.

In 1543 and 1544, Charles V of the Holy Roman

Empire pressured Countess Anna of Oldenburg not to protect the Anabaptists in her region, but to punish them harshly. She ignored him, and the Catholic church excommunicated her. Countess Anna then issued a decree saying that the Anabptists were to leave the country and that anyone who sheltered them would be punished. It is in this 1544 document that the term "Mennists" first appears to differentiate between the violent Anabaptists and the followers of Menno. The name stuck and was eventually adopted by the Swiss and South German Anabaptists as well. Meanwhile, however, Countess Anna never enforced the mandates strictly, and she remained friendly toward the Mennonites.

Menno accomplished much in his role as a leader, but it never seemed to go to his head. He was compassionate and respectful of the members of the congregations, calling them "brothers" and "sisters" in his letters. In some of his letters, he referred to himself as "the one who is lame" or "the cripple who loves you." Scholars believe he suffered a stroke that left him disabled, and several paintings of him portray him with a crutch. (See *Through Fire and Water,* pages 113-115.)

As you talk with your youth about the qualities of a leader in this session, several characteristics of Menno would be good to highlight: 1) He left a comfortable life because he was called by God to lead the Anabaptists. This role was difficult, and any glory and fame that it brought him was more than offset by the hassles and frustrations it brought him and his family. 2) Menno was a humble leader. He really was a "servant of all." 3) Menno had a physical disability. Sometimes we think that leaders have to look a certain way—that being good-looking or beautiful is part of their leadership attraction. We need to reconsider that assumption.

HANDOUT
Menno, This Is Your Life

MENNO, *This is Your Life!*

A DRAMA

CHARACTERS:
Menno
Menno's wife Gertrude
Menno's older daughter
Menno's younger daughter
Menno's son
Dutch friend
Friends of Menno (the remainder of the class—assign these parts so everyone in the class has one, or double up as needed)

Menno is sitting in a chair, reading his Bible. He is alone in the room (the stage area). The crutches are on the floor beside him. Menno falls asleep in the chair.

Gertrude walks into the room, followed by the others. They line up in front of him while she taps him on the shoulder.

Gertrude:	Menno dear, wake up.
Menno:	(*wakes up slowly; his eyes get big as he sees the people in front of him*) What in the world?
Older daughter:	You didn't think we'd forget your birthday, Dad, did you?
Everyone else:	Happy Birthday! Happy Birthday!!
Menno:	Oh my, what a surprise! I'm just an old man. You shouldn't have!
Menno's son:	Why of course we should. It's your 65th birthday!
Younger daughter:	(*pretends to show him a cake*) See, we even baked a cake!
Friend:	And that's not all. We're going to play "This is your life."
Friend:	We're going to test your memory, old man.
Menno:	Oh no!
Younger daughter:	So which do you want first—the cake or the game?

Menno:	How about cake and no game?
Son:	Not an option. Let the game begin!
Friend:	Menno, do you remember when we first met?
Menno:	Sure! You were one of the first Anabaptists that I knew. Thanks to you and some of your friends, I've been running from the government for almost 25 years, rather than having the cushy life of a priest.
Friend:	Do you regret it?
Menno:	No, no. Not at all.
Gertrude:	Well I'm glad to hear that—because we wouldn't be married if you were still a priest!
Friend:	Do you remember when a couple of us came to you and asked you to lead our group?
Menno:	I do. I refused.
Friend:	You said you needed time to think and pray about it.
Menno:	It wasn't an easy decision. If the government caught me, I could lose my life. Leading a group of persecuted people isn't something a guy does without thinking long and hard about it, and praying a lot.
Friend:	We came to you a second time, and I'll never forget what you said. Remember?
Menno:	The lost sheep need a shepherd.
Friend:	We were confused and without direction or organization. We needed someone to help us understand the Bible and help us form new congregations. We were so happy when you said yes.
Older daughter:	I must admit, there were many times when we as a family weren't so thrilled with what Dad did. We moved constantly because we had to hide from the government. And the places we stayed—yuk! Mostly they were cold and damp caves and basements.
Menno:	I've always felt bad that my calling meant such a hard life for my family.
Son:	We weren't alone, Dad. Many Anabaptists were being punished.
Friend:	How true. Remember my brother?
Menno:	How could I forget? He was killed for reading something that I wrote.
Gertrude:	And there was that man who gave you a place to hide. The government caught up with him and killed him too.
Friend:	We wanted to publish your writings so people could read them and understand about our faith. But even that meant trouble. My father was killed because he published your works.
Menno:	So much bloodshed. You don't know how many times I asked God if this was really what I should be doing. But every time, I felt such a strong conviction in my heart that I knew the answer was yes.
Friend:	There's a very funny story that has been told about you for years, Menno. You know which one I'm talking about?
Menno:	Probably the stagecoach story.
Friend:	Right. What I want to know is, is it true?

Menno (*laughing*):	I think my memory is failing me now.
Younger daughter:	Tell it again—it's such a good story.
Friend:	Apparently Menno was traveling from one place to another, as usual, trying to stay in hiding. Rather than sitting inside the stage-coach, he was riding up front, up high with the driver. The government officials stopped the stagecoach and asked, "Is Menno Simons in that coach?" Menno turned around and yelled into the coach "Is Menno Simons in there?" The passengers said, "No, he's not in here." Then Menno looked right at the authorities and said "They say Menno's not in the coach." The authorities rode away, and everyone in the coach had a good laugh. Isn't that right, Menno?
Menno:	Like I said, my memory isn't what it used to be.
Dutch Friend:	Well then, Menno, you probably don't remember me. It was nearly 20 years ago in Holland that we met. You ordained me.
Menno:	Now you are worth remembering! Of course I do! It was so exciting for me to see you taking leadership in your congregation. How's it going?
Dutch Friend:	We are growing, thanks be to God. Growing, but still being persecuted. You are fortunate to be living here in northern Germany where it's fairly safe. And what's this I hear—your home is called Menno Hut? Any relation to Pizza Hut?
Menno:	Pizza? We're not in Italy, my brother! And don't look at me—I didn't name it Menno Hut.
Son:	I guess we're responsible for that.
Dutch Friend:	And what did I see next to the house? A building with a printing press?
Menno:	God has been good. He has made it possible for the word to be spread and translated into other languages.
Friend:	How's your health, Menno?
Menno:	I get around with some help. (*He lifts up crutches.*) And not being able to walk very far has its advantages—people put me in a wagon and take me places that others would have to walk. My health is good enough for what I need to do for my Lord.
Friend:	You are a famous man, my friend. How does it feel to have a whole group of people named after you and known as the Mennists?
Menno:	It's very humbling. It's only God's grace that has made me his servant and the servant of his people.
Son:	I think we've played "This is your life" long enough, right, Dad? How about some cake?
Menno:	I thought you'd never ask.

SESSION 10
PREPARATION

ONE FOUNDATION

Scripture text: 1 Corinthians 3:10-15

Key verse: For no one can lay any foundations other than the one that has been laid; that foundation is Jesus Christ. (1 Corinthians 3:11)

Faith focus: Jesus Christ is the foundation and center for the faith and life of Christians.

Session goal: Help youth understand how central Jesus Christ is in the beliefs and practices of Menno Simons and the Mennonites today.

Materials and advance preparation
- One deck of cards for every four or five youth in the class (Focus, Option 1)
- Building blocks or bricks with statements from "Hear and Enter" either taped or written on them
- Paper, markers, and Scotch tape
- Cake and/or other snacks for a celebration at the end
- Make final arrangements for the congregational event, "About Those Anabaptists."

EXPLORATION

Option 1: Divide youth into groups of 4 or 5 and have each group build a house of cards.

Option 2: Ask for volunteers who want to build a human pyramid, OR ask the group to imagine building a pyramid with class members. Who would be placed where in the pyramid, and why?

FOCUS
(5 minutes)

Whether the group built houses of cards or a pyramid or imagined building a pyramid, discuss the following: What was the first step? (A solid base or foundation.) If the foundation wasn't solid, would you be able to build on it? What happens when part of the foundation is taken away? Have you ever done a construction or art project that didn't have a proper

CONNECT
(5 minutes)

beginning, so that the rest of the project went wrong? (Share stories if possible.)

HEAR AND ENTER
(20 minutes)

1. Read 1 Corinthians 3:10-15. Ask the youth what the passage has to do with the activity they just completed. (They were building something on a foundation. Paul used the analogy of building a house to talk about the church. For both, it's important to build a solid foundation. If our spiritual life and our faith is not built on Jesus, Paul said, then it will collapse.)

2. Build a "Menno Hut." Say: *We learned in the last lesson that Menno Simons lived the last years of his life in Germany in a house called Menno Hut. We are now going to build a Menno Hut, using as "bricks" the things we know about Menno Simons.*

Ask each youth to pick up one or more building blocks or bricks bearing the statements on page 89. Tell them that as a group, it is their job to build a "hut" from the bricks. The foundation should be made up of the statement or statements that are the strongest and most important to the structure of the hut. The statements on the tear-out sheet should be taped or written on the wood or bricks, one statement per brick.

After the youth have built their hut, discuss where they put the statements. What is the most important thing about Menno Simons? Talk about how he began his writings with 1 Corinthians 3:11: "For no one can lay any foundation other than the one that has been laid: that foundation is Jesus Christ."

APPLY
(10 minutes)

Tell students that they have discussed the "Menno Hut," and now they will be building their "Church Hut." Divide them into small groups and divide the bricks or blocks among the groups. Each group should have a marker, paper and Scotch tape. They are to write a statement for each block that shows that your congregation has its foundation built on Jesus Christ. The new statements should then be taped over the Menno statements. You may give some examples, but allow the youth to think about this and see what they come up with. This could be quite revealing as to what they perceive from your congregational life. Possible examples of statements:
We tell others about Jesus.
We pray to Jesus.

We have a Food Pantry because Jesus said we should care for the hungry.

RESPOND
(5 minutes)

This is the last session, so celebrate! Bring a cake or other snacks, throw a party! Before they can party, however, ask the youth for one more response. Go around the group and ask each person to answer the following: What difference has this series of lessons made in your life? What have you learned?

Pray before you eat, thanking God for the solid foundation of faith we have in Jesus Christ.

Option: Plan and invite your congregation to a night of "About Those Anabaptists" (See Appendix A).

REFLECT

Did the youth understand that Jesus, not any of the Anabaptists we have studied, is the foundation of our faith? Were they able to identify ways that your congregation has its foundation built upon Jesus?

Review the study as a whole. What would be an appropriate follow-up to this series? Which students were especially keen on the events and personalities of the Anabaptist movement? How can you encourage them to learn more? Which youth made significant commitments during this study? How can your affirm them and encourage their growth?

DIGGING DEEPER

Menno Simons' favorite verse points to the basis of Mennonite faith: "For no one can lay any foundation other than the one that has been laid; that foundation is Jesus Christ" (1 Cor. 3:15). This, of course, is the foundation that most Christians claim, so in that sense, the Mennonite story is part of the larger story of the Christian church. As governments and churches have become increasingly separated in recent centuries, the tension that once existed between Anabaptists and the state churches has mostly disappeared. Despite continuing differences on many of the same issues they argued about in the 16th century, Mennonites can, and often do, develop bonds of fellowship with Lutherans and Catholics around their common commitment to Christ's lordship.

Still, those who find their faith roots in the Anabaptist movement have often understood Christ's lordship somewhat differently than do some other traditions. Anabaptists have understood Jesus' Sermon on the Mount, for example, to be guidance for all Christians, here and now—not an outline for some future ideal world, or a way of life reserved only for certain Christians such as clergy and monks. In particular, the teaching on loving one's enemies has been a cornerstone for Mennonites in their refusal to take up arms. The Sermon's words on taking oaths, similarly, has led Mennonites to simply "affirm" when taking the witness stand in court. Mennonites, therefore, often place more emphasis on "following Christ" than on following the rituals and teachings of the church.

In their eagerness to follow Jesus, Anabaptists had to become keen students of the Bible. Uneducated Anabaptists were so closely connected to the story of Scripture that they could debate leading theologians of the time. It is important that we continue to find ways to tell this story to each generation, keeping it fresh and vital in our hearts and lives.

Salvation, said the Anabaptists, is more than peace between God and the individual—it also brings healing and hope into the world. This "horizontal" outgrowth of a "vertical" connection means that our relationships with each other are different because we follow Jesus. It means a commitment to serve others in practical ways, and to share the gospel with them. Where there is hatred, we seek to sow love. Where there is injury, we offer pardon. Where there is doubt, we pray for faith. Where there is despair, we bring hope. Where there is darkness, we call for God's light. Where there is sadness, we live in the joy of the Lord. We follow a Lord who gave his life, knowing that it is in dying that we are born to eternal life.

We hope this series has helped your youth not only learn about the Anabaptist and Mennonite story, but also to want to continue that story in their lives. For some, it will have reinforced some of what they might have learned earlier in their family or church. For others it will be new. It is our hope and prayer, however, that all the participants will join the Anabaptist adventure today—which ultimately means deciding to build their lives on the foundation of Jesus Christ.

HANDOUT
Menno Hut Statements

MENNO HUT STATEMENTS

(Cut out and place on the building blocks for "Hear and Enter.")

He lived in Holland for the first part of his life.

He moved to Germany where he was safer and the persecution wasn't as bad.

He was trained as a Catholic priest.

He wrote and preached about the Lord's Supper, faith, nonresistance, repentance, baptism, and the authority of the Bible.

He joined the Anabaptists and later became their leader in Holland.

His teachings went against the government and he was often being hunted.

He helped struggling Anabaptist churches get organized.

He tried to get the government to recognize the difference between the peaceful Anabaptists and those who had been violent.

He founded new churches.

People respected him.

He was a humble person and admitted he wasn't always a good servant of God.

He published his writings and also translated them so more people could understand them.

His theme in his writings and teaching was "No one can lay any foundation other than the one already laid, which is Jesus Christ."

APPENDIX A
ABOUT THOSE ANABAPTISTS

A Congregational Activity

This quiz game offers a way for your congregation to learn about the Anabaptists and at the same time reinforce what your youth have learned in the study over the last 10 sessions. Plan to do it as an extension of the last session, or as a special separate event close to the end of the sessions. You may wish to connect it to another church event, such as a potluck or even a worship service. It should take about 45 minutes.

You may wish to enhance this event by presenting one or two of the skits or readings that you did in class.

Materials and advance preparation needed:
1. Appoint a timer.
2. Appoint a master of ceremonies—preferably someone like yourself who knows enough basics of the Anabaptist story to be able to elaborate a little on some of the answers.
3. Appoint one or two people to keep track of who "rings their bell" first, and to record the scores.
4. Handouts from Adventures for background
5. Prizes (optional)
6. Refreshments

To Begin:
Divide the people into several intergenerational groups that include children, youth, and adults numbering at least 10 people per group. Each group should do the following in preparation for the game:
1. Choose four representatives who will answer the questions. If possible, one of those persons should be a youth.
2. Choose one young person to be their "bell."
3. Choose the name of a well-known Anabaptist for their group. (Menno Simons is excluded.) Examples: the Grebels, the Blaurocks, the Manzes, the Sattlers. They should be prepared to tell what they know about this person. Make available the handouts from this course for background information.

The Game Rules:

1. A team consists of four representatives from a group. When there are questions for kids only, the team should get a child from their group to answer. (Not youth who have taken the Adventures with the Anabaptists class.)

2. The MC will read the questions, and the first team to sound the bell gets the chance to answer. "Sounding the bell" occurs by a team member touching the "bell person," who then makes a bell sound. If the first team's answer is wrong, the next team to sound the bell has a chance.

3. If none of the teams know the answer, they may then turn to the rest of their group to see if they can come up with the answer. Again, the first one to sound the bell gets to answer.

4. The team with the most points at the end wins.

The Game

MC announces he or she will begin the quiz questions.

1. **Who began the Protestant Reformation in Germany almost 500 years ago?**
   A. Martin Luther (5 points)

2. **Why was it called the Protestant Reformation?**
   A. It was based on a protest. People were *protesting* against the way things were in the Catholic church in the 16th century. (5 points)

3. **Name a person, other than Martin Luther, who is a Protestant.**
   A. Of course there are many answers. Christians who are not Roman Catholic or Orthodox are usually called Protestant today. (5 points)

4. **Switzerland was the country where another Protestant Reformer, who was influenced by Martin Luther, began to raise some significant questions. His name and his city begin with the same letter. Who was it?**
   A. Ulrich Zwingli from Zurich   (10 points)

5. **(For children only) Think about the letter on the opposite end of the alphabet from the one that begins Zwingli and**

Zurich. Now, think about some people that we are going to talk about today whose name begins with that letter. Who were they?
A. Anabaptists (5 points)

6. **Explain the relationship between the Catholic church, the Protestant church, and the Anabaptists in 1525.**
A. The Protestant Reformation was a movement away from the Catholic church. The Swiss Anabaptists in Zurich broke away from the Protestants. Both the Catholics and the Protestants throughout Europe were opposed to the Anabaptists. (15 points)

7. **When and where did the Anabaptist movement begin, and what was the event that we call the beginning of that movement?**
A. The movement began in 1525, in Zurich, Switzerland, when George Blaurock asked Conrad Grebel to baptize him. (5 points for the date, 5 for the place, 5 for the event)

8. **Is there anyone here who might be called "blaurock"? Who might that be?**
A. Someone who is wearing a blue coat (or a blue shirt or blouse) (5 points)

9. **What was it about the Anabaptists and their beliefs that made the rest of the church persecute them?**
A. Mainly their belief in adult versus infant baptism (10 points) Give 5 points to those who mention the Anabaptist' insistence that the bread and cup of communion were symbols of Christ, not his literal body and blood.

10. **Why didn't the Anabaptists want to baptize babies?**
A. Because they believed that people should be old enough to understand their commitment to Christ when they were baptized, and they did not read anywhere in the Bible that infants should be baptized. (10 points)

11. **(For children only) If you have seen someone being baptized, tell us about it.**

Why was it so special? (10 points to any of the groups whose kids tell about seeing a baptism.)

12. **What was the Schleitheim Confession, where did it happen, and who was the person who wrote it?**
    A. A list of statements that summarized what the Anabaptists believed. It happened at a secret meeting of Anabaptists in the town of Schleitheim, Switzerland. Michael Sattler wrote it. (10 points for each part of the answer that they get right)

13. **Michael Sattler's wife was very involved in the Anabaptist movement, along with her husband. What was her name?**
    A. Margaretha   (5 points)

14. **How did Michael and Margaretha Sattler die?**
    A. Michael's sentence read like this: "You shall take him to the square and there first cut out his tongue, then forge him fast to a wagon, and there with glowing iron tongs twice tear pieces from his body, then on the way to the site of the execution five times more as above, and then burn his body to powder as an arch-heretic." Margaretha was drowned eight days later. (10 points for each answer)

15. **(For children only) What is a martyr?**
    A. Someone who is willing to suffer or die for his or her beliefs (5 points)

16. **What is the *Martyrs Mirror*?**
    A. A large book of true stories about Christian and Anabaptist martyrs. Next to the Bible, it was for many years the most widely read book in Mennonite homes. (5 points)

17. **Tell us the story of Dirk Willems.**
    A. Anabaptist in Holland. He was being pursued by the authorities and ran across a frozen lake. When his pursuer fell through the ice, Dirk turned around, and saved him. Even so, Dirk was arrested and eventually lost his life as a martyr. (15 points)

18. **(For children only) What group of people is named after Menno Simons?**
A. Mennonites   (5 points)

19. **Menno Simons was a priest in Holland who believed one thing but practiced another thing for 11 years. Which part of this statement is not true?**
A. The statement is all true. (15 points)

20. **Listen to the following descriptions of Menno Simons' life and choose which one is correct:**
   a. He led a group of Anabaptists who escaped persecution in Holland and moved to Germany.
   b. He was an Anabaptist leader whose strong witness when he died as a martyr was so impressive that the people who watched it decided to carry on his name and began calling themselves the Mennonites.
   c. He was a hunted man with a price on his head, so he and his family moved from place to place as he organized, led, and preached to the Anabaptists.
   d. Nobody knew him very well or met him personally, but his many writings were so inspiring to the struggling Anabaptists that they began to use his name to identify themselves.

   A. The answer is c, but there are elements of truth in some of the other statements. The MC should draw attention to the following facts about Menno: He did spend the first part of his life in Holland, but eventually made his home in Germany, but even there he was harassed for his work. Unlike many other well-known Anabaptists, he did not die a martyr's death—he lived to be an old man. He did a lot of writing and even had his own printing press.

21. **(For kids or youth only) Anabaptists in the past, and Mennonites today, are best-known for two things that make them different from many other Christians. One is believer's baptism. What is the other one?**
A. Their belief in nonviolence and peacemaking   (5 points)

22. **Teams, meet with your group and decide on a story of peacemaking that you have heard or participated in, and tell it. This question will be judged on who has the best story, not who tells theirs first.** (Rank the stories, giving 20, 15, 10, and 5 points.)

23. **Tell us everything you know about the person for whom your group is named.** (15 points for each group—unless you need a tie breaker, then use this as the tie breaker)

Declare the winning team, and give prizes if you wish. Celebrate with refreshments.

APPENDIX B

Additional Resources

Baergen, Rudy. *The Mennonite Story*. Newton, Kan.: Faith and Life Press, 1981.

Bainton, Roland H. *The Reformation of the Sixteenth Century*. Boston: The Beacon Press, 1952.

Dyck, Cornelius J. *An Introduction To Mennonite History*. Scottdale, Pa.: Herald Press, 1967, 1981, 1993.

Estep, William R. *The Anabaptist Story*. (Third Edition): Grand Rapids: William B. Eerdmans Publishing Company, 1996.

Jackson, Dave and Neta. *On Fire for Christ*. Scottdale, Pa.: Herald Press, 1989.

Loewen, Harry and Steven Nolt. *Through Fire and Water*. Scottdale, Pa.: Herald Press, 1996.

Smith, C. Henry. *Story of the Mennonites*. Newton, Kan.: Faith and Life Press, 1981.

Snyder, C. Arnold and Linda A. Huebert Hecht. *Profiles of Anabaptist Women*. Waterloo, Ont.: Wilfrid Laurier University Press, 1996.

The Radicals (video). Gateway Films/Vision Video, 1989.

Van Braght, Thieleman J. *Martyrs Mirror*. Scottdale, Pa.: Herald Press, 1938.

Waltner, James H. *This We Believe*. Newton, Kan.: Faith and Life Press, 1968.

Weaver, J. Denny. *Becoming Anabaptist*. Scottdale, Pa.: Herald Press, 1987.

To order books published by Herald Press and Faith & Life Resources call 1-800-245-7894 or 1-800-743-2484. Catalogs are also available.